Culture First!

Promoting Standards in the New Media Age

Edited by

Kenneth Dyson and Walter Homolka

CASSELL

Cassell
Wellington House
125 Strand
London WC2R 0BB

127 West 24th Street
New York, NY 10011

First published 1996

British Library Cataloguing-in-Publication Data
A catalogue record for this book is available from the British Library.

ISBN 0-304-33771-4 (hardback)
0-304-33772-2 (paperback)

Cover design by Ben Cracknell
Front cover cartoon by David Shenton

Typeset by Keystroke, Jacaranda Lodge, Wolverhampton
Printed and bound in Great Britain by Biddles Ltd,
Guildford and King's Lynn

Contents

Men lose their high aspirations, as they lose their intellectual tastes, because they have no time or opportunity for indulging them: and they addict themselves to inferior pleasures not because they deliberately prefer them but because they are either the only ones to which they have access or the only ones which they are any longer capable of enjoying.

John Stuart Mill, *Utilitarianism* (1861; 1962 Fontana edn, p. 261)

Contributors

Kenneth Dyson, Professor of European Studies and co-director of the European Briefing Unit, University of Bradford, United Kingdom

Wolfgang Hoffmann-Riem, Professor of Public Law and director of the Hans-Bredow Institute for Radio and Television, University of Hamburg, Germany

Walter Homolka, Doctor of Economics and of Theology, Chief of Staff to the President and Chief Executive, Bertelsmann Book Corporation, Munich, Germany

Hermann Lübbe, Professor of Philosophy and Political Theory, University of Zurich, Switzerland

Neil Postman, Professor of Media Ecology, New York University, United States

Gerhard Schulze, Professor of Empirical Social Research, University of Bamberg, Germany

Peter Winterhoff-Spurk, Professor of Organizational and Media Psychology, University of Saarbrücken, Germany, and director of the Media Psychology Research Institute there

Preface

Do we live well? Do the organization of our media and our use of the media suggest that we know how to live well? Academics, and in particular those in the fast-growing field of media studies, have on the whole been uncomfortable with the unavoidably normative language of quality. Yet with the revolutionary changes affecting media today – encapsulated in the terms 'digital revolution' and 'multimedia' – these questions have taken on an added significance. As individuals we are confronted with the problem of a vast expansion of choices in media consumption (how should we use our time?). As individuals we face a new burden of aesthetic and ethical responsibility for the quality of the media which we receive and whose production we encourage. How are we to exercise that greater responsibility? From media studies there has been little attempt to provide an answer to these types of question, though they are precisely the questions to which people want answers. This book will disappoint those who want definitive answers. It is essentially a 'map-and-compass' guide, designed to try to point people in the right direction.

From Samuel Taylor Coleridge and Matthew Arnold in the nineteenth century to Neil Postman and Richard Hoggart today it is possible to trace an intellectual tradition of cultural criticism that challenges the way in which people currently lead their lives. In this tradition can be identified a particular view of the role of philosophy: that its task is to show us how to live. The roots of this particular tradition of cultural criticism, or to be more precise literary criticism, go way back beyond the nineteenth century to classical philosophy's concern with how to practise the good life. But, as we shall see, a more immediate impetus was provided by the work of the German philosopher Immanuel Kant (1724–1804) on aesthetics, ethics and philosophy of history.

At the heart of this tradition of cultural criticism and celebration of the 'literary' intelligence were two passionately held convictions: that a 'faith in machinery', exemplified by fascination with 'technological society' and its undoubted benefits for human welfare, will not deliver the good life to us; and that, if we are to realize the good life, we must transcend our 'ordinary selves' by aspiring to the cultural standards that will enable us to better approximate to our 'best selves'. Those standards are ethical, involving an appeal to our capacity to develop and exercise moral intelligence; they are also aesthetic, pointing out that we can educate our tastes and make mature aesthetic judgements. The note of passion and *gravitas* and sense of intellectual responsibility derive from the significance that such intellectuals attach to aesthetic and ethical standards as the basis for a civilized society; and from their sense of the duty of the intellectual to protect and promote these standards and the fundamental importance of education for this purpose.

Allegiance to, or separation from, Kant is a useful indicator of underlying philosophical attitudes about the role of the intellectual and the nature of cultural criticism. Kant's critique of reason was not only a virtual 'Copernican revolution' in philosophy; its implications for the practice of cultural criticism were profound. For Kant the fundamental task was to determine the grounds of rational belief and rational action. Given that the mind was not a passive mirror to the world (as argued by British empiricists) but an active agency composing the raw material of sense experience into meaningful patterns, the prime requirement was practical rules for the purpose of controlling the world in which we live.

This premise led Kant to contrast determinate judgements with reflective judgements, each concerned with different phenomena and involving a different form of intellectual activity. Determinate judgements involve the study of cause–effect relationships and are restricted to the world of sense experience, the phenomenal order of space and time. But only a limited set of questions in media studies and cultural criticism can be addressed using the category of cause and effect. More important is the activity that Kant calls reflective judgement. Reflective judgement is concerned with how we ought to live. It is an activity of practical or moral reason, grounded in the notion of autonomous postulates of aesthetics and ethics, the idea of the authority of the conscience and the capability of man to base conduct on an act of will harmonized with reason. As we shall see in Chapter 1, postmodernists tend to lack Kant's confidence either in causal explanation or in practical reason. They prefer to celebrate how we live rather than reflect on what we ought to do, to elevate the ordinary into cultural phenomena and to practise intellectual playfulness as an end in itself instead of engaging in deeper arguments about right and wrong, good and bad.

Kant's great contribution to cultural criticism rests in the importance that he attached to distinctive criteria – aesthetic, ethical and historical – that alone provide adequate standards for assessing the validity of truth claims. These openly articulated principles and values form the basis for a process of reasoned critical enquiry. It is these fundamental tenets of Enlightenment thought that hold together the intellectual tradition of cultural criticism outlined above and distinguish it from postmodernism's fascination with 'free-floating' media images, the openness and lack of objective content of 'texts' and the power of the 'reader' to define and create textual meaning. Postmodernism's philosophical roots lie with two other German philosophers – Friedrich Nietzsche and Martin Heidegger – and their scepticism about the possibility of truth, reason and moral universals. For those in the Kantian tradition the capacity to discriminate between the ephemeral and the serious, between good and bad, was the basic requirement of the critical intellectual.

Sadly, the story of the twentieth century has been the decline of this neo-Kantian intellectual tradition of literary cultural criticism. Its robust type of intellectual has become the exception rather than the rule. One factor has been the material change in media brought about by the technologies of television and micro-electronics and by television's emergence, and increasingly the computer screen, as the central cultural stage in our societies. We live in an increasingly 'media-saturated' world in which surface and style, what things look like, and pun and parody achieve a value in their own right; in which media images and signs come increasingly to influence our sense of reality and the way in which we define ourselves in the world. Television and the computer have challenged a 'print-centred' culture and undermined the prestige of literary culture and confidence in the literary intelligence. Postman and Homolka expand this argument in this book. They point out how television, and now the computer, have changed the total context in which we experience culture, bringing with them their own distinctive values. In the process intellectual life has been radically transformed. This new technological and media context is less hospitable to the role of figures modelled on Coleridge and Arnold. Rather, it has created a new range of professional groups with a vested interest in new media: from advertisers, marketing specialists, accountants, television production people, journalists and computer graphics specialists to media studies lecturers. In celebrating media consumerism as a democratizing process postmodernism has provided these groups with an ideology that justifies their role and serves their self-interests. Postmodernism's grip comes from the basic fact that it arises from the interests of those working in, and controlling, proliferating new media.

Alongside technological change has been a whole series of intellectual developments that have conspired to make this type of neo-Kantian cultural criticism unfashionable. Marxism undermined the authority of standards by assimilating them to dominant economic élites and categorizing them as instruments of social control and propaganda: as symptomatic of ideological domination. Liberalism, with its celebration of the individual, trusted in market competition and consumer choice. The individual was the best judge of her/his own interests when it came to standards. Though the normative principles and causal beliefs of liberalism and Marxism differed radically, they could agree in seeing standards as essentially a by-product of the functioning of the 'cultural industries'. They explored the economic realities by which culture was produced/manufactured.

More recently, postmodernism has further undermined the notion of independent cultural standards in terms of which we can describe, interpret and evaluate what is happening in the media. Its practitioners insist that subjective and conflicting interpretations are the closest that we can come to understanding the world; and they share a conviction that terms like good and bad are inappropriate. Cultural meanings are made by 'active' audiences who assimilate media into their everyday lives and use them to creatively remake the world. With postmodernism comes the celebration of popular culture in all its forms, from pop videos to television advertisements and soap operas. The role of the intellectual within this framework is to reveal the layers of metaphor contained in apparently ordinary media images, thereby opening up the complex constitution and contradictions of modern culture and throwing light on wider social issues. It is to liberate lost voices and to challenge and unmask the voices who claim to represent standards, such as, for instance, those who profess to provide objectivity in news reporting.

It is unquestionably the case that concepts like the 'cultural industries' and 'active audiences' have contributed enormously to our understanding of how media function. They show us how in practice cultural standards have been economically and socially constituted, as Chapter 8 emphasizes. Media studies has gained an anchoring in some key realities of how media work. But one does not need to be a Marxist, market liberal or postmodernist to recognize and appreciate these influences. More fundamentally, economists and sociologists are not *per se* professionally well-equipped to advise on cultural standards. Their disposition is to ignore them or to expose them as myth and consign them to oblivion. It is the task of philosophy to rescue cultural standards by renewing our sense of how we should and could live: a philosophy that returns to the inspiration of Kant. By reinvigorating itself from this source media studies will be better equipped to show how aesthetics and ethics can teach us something about how to live and about the kinds of reflective judgements that intellectual enquiry should enable us to make.

Acknowledgements

A particular debt of gratitude is owed to Bertelsmann Books, to the Stiftung Lesen and to Zweites Deutsches Fernsehen (ZDF) for organizing – in September 1994 in Frankfurt – the conference on which this book draws.

The chapters by no means represent all the conference papers, and some new essays have been added. Selection has been dictated by the theme of technology and culture and by the question of the implications of current technological changes, associated with the so-called 'digital revolution', for culture. The intention has not been to provide a comprehensive overview of the scope of these changes or of the detailed way in which they are affecting the processes of 'encoding' and 'decoding' at work in broadcasting. For such material the reader can turn to various general texts. Instead, the focus is on the ethical and aesthetic implications, examined from various disciplinary perspectives: philosophical, historical, legal, political and socio-psychological. The book seeks to interest those who are passionately concerned about ethical and aesthetic standards in our cultural life, who recognize the profound cultural transformations that will come with the digital age, and who are attracted by exploring how scholars from various disciplines see the problem of cultural quality in this radically new context.

Within the University of Bradford we have been fortunate in having had first-rate secretarial assistance from Amanda Machin. In addition to the normal work of editing we have also undertaken the daunting task of translation from German into English. Accordingly, we accept full responsibility for any errors and infelicities that result from translation – an activity in which we can lay claim to no professional qualification.

Finally, but not least, our thanks to the contributors to the book for meeting editorial deadlines with such efficiency and good humour. For us the making of this volume has been yet another reminder of the pleasures and profits of Anglo-German co-operation.

Kenneth Dyson and Walter Homolka
December 1995

1

Revisiting *Culture and Anarchy*: Media Studies, the Cultural Industries and the Issue of Quality

KENNETH DYSON

Estote ergo vos perfecti! – 'the full perfection of our humanity'.[1]

The warnings of Matthew Arnold to his mid-nineteenth-century contemporaries seem to have acquired a new relevance: for, once again, society seems to be in the process of 'shooting Niagara'. The omens take various forms: new technological breakthroughs – represented by the 'digital revolution'; emerging economic forces – exemplified by the market leadership role of Rupert Murdoch in new media applications and a wave of multimedia mergers; and zealous political ideologies – in this case committed to the values of the market and strategies of deregulation and privatization of media. 'Shooting Niagara' means today what it meant for Arnold over a century ago: a loss of direction and control; a perception that culture is threatened by, and must be rescued from, technological, economic and political assaults.

Earlier in the twentieth century this sense of impending anarchy was unleashed by the development of terrestrial radio and television broadcasting. A process of reduction of cultural values to the lowest common denominator seemed to be suggested by broadcasters' cultivation of a 'mass' audience and by the influence of commercial techniques (like the ratings system) and commercial ownership on programme production and programming strategies. In Britain, for instance, the Pilkington Committee of 1962 castigated the 'triviality' of the new commercial broadcasting channel, ITV. As the twenty-first century approached, the birth of 'multimedia' suggested a further profound transformation, driven again by technology and economics, but with little attention to its cultural content and implications. The shock of technological innovation has repeatedly drawn forth an impassioned debate about cultural standards.

'Culture and anarchy'

Even if the past has never been a reliable guide to the future, it is instructive to look back beyond the age of radio and television to one of the towering figures of mid-nineteenth-century debate about culture and material progress – Matthew Arnold. As the apostle of 'culture and poetry', in the face of the omens of 'anarchy' associated with 'shooting Niagara' in his England of the 1860s, his celebration of the values of literary culture and his mockery of dismal Philistinism have a renewed relevance in the context of current changes and debate about 'quality'. For Arnold the besetting dangers of mid-Victorian England were a 'faith in machinery', in the mechanical and external condition of our civilization, and a faith in our freedom to say and do just what we like, following the dictates of our 'ordinary selves'. Crucial to Arnold was the insight that culture fosters the internal growth of our humanity; that we have a 'best self' as well as an 'ordinary self', based on a commitment to 'a growing and a becoming' as opposed to expressing our animality; that culture tries to develop in us that 'best self' at the expense of 'our old untransformed self', to open up to us the insight that there is something wiser than our ordinary selves:[2]

> But culture indefatigably tries, not to make what each raw person may like, the rule by which he fashions himself: but to draw ever nearer to a sense of what is indeed beautiful, graceful and becoming, and to get the raw person to like that.[3]

In Arnold's famous definition, culture is 'a study of perfection'. It means:

> getting to know, on all the matters which most concern us, the best which has been thought and said in the world, and through this knowledge, turning a stream of fresh thought upon our stock notions and habits, which we now follow staunchly but mechanically, vainly imagining that there is virtue in following them staunchly which makes up for the mischief of following them mechanically.

Here was no attempt to rescue the high manners and grand style of a traditionally English aristocratic image of society. Arnold characterized the aristocracy as the 'Barbarians', strong in dignity and politeness but deficient in intelligence and 'light'. The middle class too were condemned for their hardness and vulgarity, as smug, self-satisfied, parochial and provincial 'Philistines', suspicious of the claims of culture; whilst the 'Populace' was too raw and blind. Culture, in Arnold's view, turned a free play of ideas on the prejudices of each and every class and intellectual faction. What was common to all factions was the assumption of their members that they should exercise their birthright of 'doing as they like', in other words of following the dictates of their 'ordinary selves'. Arnold was in effect outlining an immense cultural project of educational self-improvement, dedicated to enlarging access to 'the best which has been thought and said in the world' and to 'turning a stream of fresh and free thought upon our stock notions and habits'. The duty of 'the men of culture' was to civilize and humanize classes and factions and, in the process, to act as 'the true apostles of equality', spreading the values of sound learning, literary criticism and poetic imagination.

Arnold was clear about the institutional context that was indispensable if we were to be enabled to transcend our lower, ordinary selves and attend to the life of the spirit: making the idea of the state and the idea of the university central in national life as the organs of culture and the best self, serving an ideal higher than that of the ordinary man. With this sense of moral purpose went an unease about the effects of extending the electoral franchise and a sense that representation of the people was in itself no adequate guarantee of civilized conduct. As he noted in *Culture and Anarchy*, 'Our whole scheme of government being representative, every one of our governors has all possible temptation, instead of setting up before the governed who elect him . . . a high standard of right reason, to accommodate himself as much as possible to their natural taste for the bathos'. Arnold would have felt a similar unease about placing too much faith in media consumerism as a guarantee of cultural standards.

He was also clear that poetic sensibility was at the very heart of cultural experience. Poetic imagination is the unique inspirer of conduct, moving, penetrating and transforming the individual: the very essence of aesthetic experience.

> More and more mankind will discover that we have to turn to poetry to interpret life for us, to console us, to sustain us. Without poetry, our science will appear incomplete; and most of what now passes with us for religion and philosophy will be replaced by poetry.[4]

Arnold's insistence on discrimination between the good, the bad and the indifferent as the fundamental task of the critic finds its echo in

contemporary debate about cultural standards in the media.[5] There
are those who remind us that there is such a thing as a judgement
of quality as distinct from audience ratings and that this judgemental thinking involves reference to independent aesthetic criteria;
that the cultural purpose of the media is to foster critical literacy
rather than to take basic literacy as its standard; and that there is a
distinction between 'populist' programmes that target audience
share and advertisers and 'popular' programmes that use drama or
comedy to offer wider and deeper insights into the world. Arnold
would have sympathized passionately with these arguments and
identified in the dominant language of public relations, accountancy
and advertising in modern media the contemporary 'Philistines'. The
age of multimedia presents itself *par excellence* as the embodiment
of the 'faith in machinery' and in 'doing as one pleases'.

The debate about quality in contemporary media studies: the problems of postmodernism

Contemporary media studies have, on the whole, proved deeply
resistant to engagement in normative debates about quality and to
the idea of championing particular aesthetic and ethical standards.
There have been some important exceptions, typically having their
intellectual roots in those branches of literary criticism that continue
to celebrate the autonomy of cultural texts and the importance
of their close reading. This general reluctance to train and exercise
judgement about right and wrong, good and bad, has its roots in a
shift in the philosophical centre of gravity in the social sciences, and
in literary criticism, away from the philosophical idealism that
inspired Arnold and many of his Victorian contemporaries. Quite
simply, there is an aversion to giving priority to issues of aesthetic
and moral conduct as conceived from the perspective of a sense of
social purpose and direction. This philosophic shift in turn reflects
deeper economic, social and cultural changes that are bound up with
the advent of information and communication technologies and the
rise of new professional and intellectual interests linked to the
exploitation of those technologies.

The preface on the thinking of Arnold about culture helps to
identify the basis of the concern about standards of cultural quality
in the media that animates this volume. At the level of intellectual
debate, the themes of a distinction between our 'best self' and our

'ordinary self' and of a public interest in promoting ethical standards and aesthetic perceptiveness, and the standards of independent judgement associated with that perceptiveness, have been subordinated to other interests. Within intellectual debate about media culture Arnold would have identified factions similar to those he attacked in the mid-nineteenth century: the academic 'Philistines', earnest in their 'faith in machinery' but lacking in 'sweetness and light', and those (the postmodernists) who speak as the tribunes of the 'Populace', celebrating media culture from the perspective of its audiences and 'demythologizing' standards of objectivity and cultural excellence in favour of multiple wisdoms and cultures and a relativism of knowledge.[6] For him, the last main testament of the 'men of culture' would remain the report of the Pilkington Committee on Broadcasting in 1962. Here there was at least an attempt to be explicit about judgements of quality, not least in its conclusion that 'triviality is a natural vice of television':

> A trivial presentation may consist in a failure to take full and disciplined advantage of the artistic and technical facilities which are relevant to a particular subject, or in a reliance on 'gimmicks' so as to give a spurious interest to a programme at the cost of its imaginative integrity, or in too great a dependence on hackneyed devices for creating suspense or raising a laugh or evoking tears . . . Programmes which exemplified emotional tawdriness and mental timidity helped to cheapen both emotional and intellectual values.[7]

Tendencies to Philistinism and to settle for playing the role of tribune of the Populace are apparent within the intellectual field that appears to be ascendant in media studies – sociology. Its key modern constitutive and contending elements – most notably, a residual Marxism, structuralism, and postmodernism – have epistemological roots wholly different from those of Arnold and those who reflect on culture from within the philosophical tradition that he represents. The sociological perspective on culture is well captured in the following quotation:

> Taste and style are socially and culturally determined. It is the power to decide upon the definitions of taste and style which circulate within societies which is important, rather than the remote possibility of finding universal and objective reasons for validating aesthetic judgements.[8]

Marxism, ideology and the Frankfurt School

It is difficult to underestimate the influence of Marxism on basic assumptions within contemporary cultural studies. Fundamental to Marxist accounts is the notion that to understand cultural texts and practices one must attend to the material conditions of their production and the economic relations within which this production takes place. In Marxism-based sociological argument cultural standards are seen as pre-eminently a manifestation of values learnt and transmitted by the class system. Hence to argue for cultural standards in the media is to risk aligning oneself with the dominant interests in a class society, to adopt the view 'from above' about the importance of hierarchy and conformity in ensuring that the media contribute to social order. For theorists like Pierre Bourdieu, the social function of aesthetics is to make class-based and culture-specific differences of taste appear universal and therefore natural.[9] Its content reflects the differential possession of 'cultural capital' as determined by economic position and social status. Aesthetic judgements involve the reproduction of privilege, typically in the form of inherited cultural capital acquired unconsciously via family and educational environment.

One particularly influential concept within media studies has been hegemony, associated with the legacy of Antonio Gramsci. It is seen in the argument that the function of the ethics of news, current affairs and documentary programmes is propaganda. They manufacture consent by mobilizing support for the special interests that dominate the state and private-sector activity.[10] Media are one, increasingly important, means by which dominant groups strive to secure the consent of subordinate groups to their leadership. Alongside, or in place, of coercion, social order rests on elements of consent and consensus based on the production, distribution and interpretations of ideas and knowledge by intellectuals. In short, intellectuals are best conceived as engaged in the establishment of hegemony and conflicts about that hegemony. With Gramsci culture succeeds in establishing a measure of importance in its own right by breaking free of the shackles of a Marxian economic determinism. But it remains essentially an aspect of social control and class-based action.[11]

Gramsci's concept of hegemony was crucial in establishing the notion of culture as a terrain in which a continuing ideological struggle takes place about meaning. Culture became inherently ideological, in other words was to be thought about politically. Within this framework Stuart Hall developed a theory of 'articulation' to explain the processes of ideological struggle.[12] He argued that cultural texts and practices were not inscribed with meaning by the intentions of their producers. Meaning is always the result of an act of 'articulation', an act of active production in use; its expression connected to, and conditioned by, a specific historical context. Hence a cultural text or practice is not the issuing source of meaning but a site where the articulation of various meanings takes place. Culture is, in short, a site where hegemony is to be won or lost.

The conception of culture as an instrument of social control was given a pessimistic form in the neo-Marxism of the Frankfurt School. A notable exponent was Herbert Marcuse, who argued that the combination of new media technologies with the manipulations and seductions of contemporary affluent societies had reduced culture to an instrumental, machine-like function for promoting social order.[13] This particularly crude type of Marxism contrasts with the more important work of Theodor Adorno on aesthetics and literary criticism. For Adorno too power resided with the culture industry and its twin processes of standardization and 'pseudo-individualization'. Originality and intellectual stimulation were squeezed out by the economics of cultural production, which in turn exploited peripheral frills, novelties and stylistic variations to make cultural products appear new and different, in the process disguising the underlying standardization. The power of the cultural industry expressed itself in its capacity to shape and perpetuate a 'regressive' audience of dependent, passive and servile consumers who behave like children.[14]

But Adorno's contribution lies in his effort to save difficult art and philosophy from the homogenizing effects of commercialization, from the process by which cultural objects are reduced to exchange-value and thus the status of a 'mere object'. The cultural object as aesthetic experience has to be preserved from its equation with price and reduction to 'commodity fetishism'. The means to achieve this result lie in the promotion of the avant-garde, challenging people to understand that the work of art is a complex *tour de force*. Here was an attempt to reconcile Marxism with the notion of a boundary between art and popular culture.[15]

More perceptive still, and later influential within postmodernist circles, was Walter Benjamin's work, which offered an astute analysis of a fundamental change in the context within which we view the aesthetic quality of works of art.[16] Benjamin argued that new technological processes of reproduction (he was writing in the context of photography, the phonograph, radio and the cinema) were destroying the mystique and authority of works of art. In bringing works of art closer to a mass audience by making images generally available, and by bypassing the difference between original and copy, new media were endowing works of art with an ephemeral quality and undermining their value. One consequence was a change in the creative process itself; works of art were now designed for reproducibility, opening up new aesthetic potentialities. Another consequence was that, with the possibility of reproducibility, a work of art can be endowed with meaning from a diversity of different contexts. This insight was to be crucial later in postmodernist exploitation of pastiche, collage and montage to provoke new readings. Another legacy to postmodernism came in the form of Benjamin's argument that the film audience occupies the same position as the camera. Hence it may have an active role in the viewing of a film. Benjamin's work also opened up the question of how new techniques of art, like film, change our field of perception, sensitizing us to aspects of our environment (via, for instance, close-ups) that were hitherto unnoticed.

Structuralism

There was a significant cross-over between Marxism and structuralism, with each motivated by the search to situate specific phenomena in a wider social whole and to identify causal explanations. Structuralist accounts stressed that cultural phenomena were not objective facts identifiable by their inherent properties. They were purely 'relational' entities, deriving their identity and meaning from the wider system of signs, codes and rules that each person has unconsciously imbibed in a given society and that structure their interpretations. Structuralism also involved certain claims about the universal character of mental and cultural structures and their causal effects in giving rise to certain observable phenomena, like myths. The key task was to identify and analyse the underlying signifying structures in terms of which the competent reader or viewer 'decodes' cultural forms like television programmes, but stressing all the time an essentially deterministic view of the reader or viewer.[17] This activity involved a cross-over between sociology and linguistics, drawing heavily on semiology which is concerned with studying how human beings communicate, or attempt to communicate, by signs (whether language, gestures, music, clothes, food, advertisements or other artefacts). The aim was to provide a truly 'scientific' study of cultural texts and practices, focusing on the nature of the 'signifier' and the 'signified' contained within a sign and understanding them in terms of the wider system of signs of which they are a part.

The result was an evolution of a new elaborate terminology and categorization in cultural studies and an exceptional verbal and theoretical aptitude among its exponents. Simple things were read in the most complex of ways; new opportunities opened up for intellectual playfulness. But, in the process, the capacity to discriminate in aesthetic and ethical terms and the notion of individual responsibility for such discrimination were devalued. This devaluation was accompanied by some questionable assumptions about the 'system' of language as something independent of the contexts in which people use it and about the capacity to interpret signs without reference to those contexts and the social relationships which confer meaning on them.[18]

Postmodernism

With poststructuralism, and notably postmodernism, comes a subversion of key structuralist views: that texts retain an objective status; that they instruct readers; and that interpretation is controlled by impersonal linguistic and literary codes ('reading' being an impersonal activity). Central to poststructuralism, and its key legacy to postmodernism, was the idea that language constitutes, rather than reflects, reality. Hence the central task was to expose the workings of language and its shortcomings in exposing anything outside itself. One main strand of poststructuralism was provided by discourse analysis which – following Michel Foucault – focused on the study of media language as a means of revealing how knowledge is organized to construct and control audiences, for instance by the way in which audiences are constructed or women represented.[19] The power of television institutions is apparent in the way in which they control their audiences by treating them as objects of discourses.

A politics of knowledge is at work in television; and the task of the intellectual is to show how that politics works and to work against the hegemony of any single discursive system.[20] Another strand was reader-response criticism, which argued that meanings are the 'production' or 'creation' of the individual reader rather than features of the work itself.[21] Roland Barthes and others proclaimed the 'death of the author'. In these sorts of ways poststructuralism contributed to postmodernism.

Postmodernism can be seen as an attempt to come to terms with the advent of information technology and a media-saturated world. For commentators like Jean Baudrillard representations have come to create rather than reflect reality in the world of electronic media, becoming endowed with an almost material status. 'Signs', 'simulations' and the 'code' are the most important constitutive elements in the contemporary world (if not the only ones). They follow their own independent logic, above all the digital code of the information technology age which has raised simulation to an unprecedented importance in social life. The 'era of the code', with its logic of reproduction and simulation (note here an influence from Benjamin), has begun to penetrate the whole of the social fabric. In this information-saturated world meaning, depth and authenticity are disappearing, to be replaced by a 'plethora of floating signifiers'. Reality is reduced to simulacra; the 'hyperreal' (*reproduced* reality) displaces the real; and the distinction between 'public space' and 'private space' disappears.[22] This upgrading of the importance of culture endows those who work in producing culture and studying culture with a new role and legitimacy, a not unimportant factor in explaining the appeal and success of postmodernism as ideology. It also undermined the claims of Marxism to offer a convincing account of the information technology, 'media-saturated' modern (or rather postmodern) age. What is on offer is a bleak picture of a potentially closed system of 'imploding meaning' in which opposites begin to collapse and matters of aesthetics and ethics become undecidable.

As far as postmodernism in media studies was concerned the work of de Certeau was highly influential. His work departs from Baudrillard's notion of us as the helpless victims of a technological determinism, absorbing the masses and leaving them only with a counter-strategy of indifference. By focusing on the practice of everyday life de Certeau sought to uncover the widespread popular resistance to the existing social order to be found in daily and apparently ordinary media consumption, showing how the consumer 'poached' media products and engaged in 'guerilla tactics'. Television culture took on the quality of a 'semiotic democracy'.[23]

This celebration of the liberating potential of media consumerism was further explored in the work of sociologists like Mike Featherstone on the roots of postmodernism in the long-term growth of a consumer culture; and in the expansion in the number of professional workers ('new cultural intermediaries') engaged in the production and distribution of symbolic goods (the 'image production industries').[24] Its social location is in the urban, affluent, well-educated 'new middle class'; its preoccupation is with 'lifestyle' and the 'aestheticization' of daily life; and its notion of the aesthetic is essentially eclectic, celebrating a range of styles and drawing on the whole repertory of art, and characterized by a 'controlled hedonism'. Postmodern aesthetics is bound up with the process of conspicuous consumption.

In essence, postmodernism as understood in literary and media studies abandons the 'author' who writes or creates a text and empowers the 'reader' who interprets the text; it broadens the notion of 'text' to include all phenomena and events, including advertisements, popular music and popular artefacts; it questions the attribution of privilege or special status to 'expert' voices in favour of the 'public' voice; it denies any independent criteria by which art can be distinguished from popular culture; and it celebrates the diverse, iconoclastic, referential and collage-like nature of cultural expression. There is heightened sense of just how varied, fragmentary and mutually contradictory are the meanings that make up culture. Culture is conceived by postmodernists as an unregulatable play of purely relational elements; no 'text' means what it seems to say but is at the mercy of its 'readers'. The postmodern world is a social space populated by relatively autonomous agents. The identities of these agents are 'neither given nor authoritatively confirmed' but the temporary outcome of a continuing process of self-assembly. Though postmodern culture permits the exercise of ethical and aesthetic choices – indeed is a challenge to the agent to become a moral subject – its theorists see this culture as essentially indeterminate. There is no confidence in independent criteria that might guide such choices; only an acceptance of confusion.[25]

For many postmodern writers the main function of theory is

adversarial rather than explanatory. This adversarial mode of post-modernism takes a number of forms. By embracing the models of 'popular culture' (music videos, television soap operas, etc.), and by blending different genres, cultural and stylistic levels, and the playful and the serious, the élitism of 'high art' is being overthrown; and, in rejecting the notion of an authoritative reading of texts, cultural criticism is engaging in a project of political resistance to mechanisms of social control.[26] Members of the television audience become producers of their own meanings according not to one code but to a multiplicity of codes. They are represented as voyeurs adrift in a sea of symbols, knowing and seeing themselves through the images of television and cinema.[27] There is no final authoritative meaning against which the correctness or truth of specific cultural readings can be judged: at best only 'interpretive communities', each of which shares a particular 'reading strategy'; or, more bleakly, the 'post-modern sublime', in which 'there is no criterion for assessing the role of taste, and so everybody is alone when it comes to judging'.[28] In short, though there is a normative tendency to celebrate the ways in which television can serve the interests of socially subordinate and oppressed groups, judgemental thinking about cultural standards is formally banished.

What unites the various critical perspectives of Marxism and the Frankfurt School, structuralism and postmodernism in sociological accounts of media culture is a shared preoccupation with the question '*whose* cultural standards?': with identifying the social agents who claim a privileged status for their cultural standards in media regulation, programme production and programming. The achievements of this literature have been formidable and must not be underestimated. It unmasked the social and economic context of the debate about cultural standards and the power relations inscribed in the way in which media function. Above all, attention was drawn to the differential possession of 'cultural capital', consequent on the educational and occupational systems and on differential access to the major institutions of learning and publicity-making.[29] Culture was conceived of as a field of relations structured by power and reproducing privilege.

With this kind of analysis came a certain liberation of cultural analysis, taking it away simply from the privileged space of artistic production and aesthetic knowledge into the 'lived experience' of everyday life, into the analysis of 'popular culture'.[30] The range of subject matter was extended radically. The cultural importance of the 'lived' experience of television soap operas, quiz shows, advertisements and music videos was opened up to investigation: both in terms of the values specific to the genre and in terms of the cultural competencies involved.[31] Significant insights were gained into alternative subcultures and cultural options, like the worlds of male youth subcultures, different ethnic groups and female cultural forms.[32] Cultural analysis was invited to give attention to pleasure: to the mundane, everyday sort of pleasure (*plaisir*) typically offered by television as a means of confirming one's sense of identity (perhaps in opposition to ideological control); and to the heightened sensuality (*jouissance*) experienced in television images.[33]

But sociological analysis of media culture had difficulty in resolving the tension between those arguing that 'texts' were to be read in terms of dominant ideology (as 'closed texts') and those pointing to the social experience of the reader/viewer as the site of cultural meanings. Drawing on and modifying the work of Stuart Hall on 'reading' theory, Fiske has sought to shift analysis in the direction of emphasizing television's 'openness', its invitations to viewers to construct their meanings out of its texts. Television viewing was characterized as a process of negotiation between the text and its various socially situated readers.[34] The result of the de Certeau/Fiske type of approach was a bias to decode popular culture in terms of opposition, resistance and empowerment (Hall's 'production in use' idea of culture). 'The culture of everyday life is best described through metaphors of struggle or antagonism . . . top-down power opposed by bottom-up power, social discipline faced with disorder.'[35]

Besides the inaccessibility of much of its language, sociology's most insidious legacy in media studies was a pervasive cultural relativism. Media standards tended to be seen as simply an attribute, expression or reflection of the culture of a set of people; the notion of critical standards independent of the entrepreneur, producer or viewer was lost from view; and the issue of citizenship – of the members of the audience as having rights of access to the full range of information, argument and interpretation that they need to act as responsible citizens – was displaced. The danger that media studies faced under its influence was a slippage from rescuing and celebrating 'ordinariness', as understood by Raymond Williams, to an exaggeration of the oppositional meaning of media consumption, a veneration of the banal, an appetite for the ephemeral, an 'uncritical populist drift' and a romantic celebration of the media consumer and of 'life as art'.[36] Sociologists tended to be fundamentally uncomfortable with attempts to apply 'unitary' cultural standards of what would be in the public interest in media: either because they feared becoming the handmaiden of social control; or because such standards seemed incompatible with the reality of 'freefloating signifiers' and social complexity, contingency, confusion and change that many of them saw as the hallmarks of postmodernity.

On closer examination the aversion to the idea of independent cultural standards appears overstated. It is possible to ground the activity of discrimination in independent criteria by reference to which the claims and behaviour of all social actors can be evaluated, including those with power over media. They are a powerful instrument of criticism whose application can be generalized to those who possess and use cultural capital, far more powerful than the activity of intellectual playfulness generated by structuralism and postmodernism. No less seriously, structuralism and postmodernism have been much stronger on theory generation than procedures of empirical validation. Postmodernism underlines some important technological and economic changes that are transforming the nature of the media that we experience and the way in which we experience the world. But their effects are being exaggerated in a way that reflects the ideological interests of those working in and studying media – and the way their lives have changed – more than the way in which most people actually interact with media. Borrowing from Baudrillard, we may be prepared to accept that the era of the digital code is penetrating our social fabric.[37] Yet we must distinguish between its role as ideology and as a characterization of an empirical phenomenon. We do not, and need not, live solely within the terms of that code.

Under the impact of trends within sociology media studies has stepped away from facing up to some of the key issues facing contemporary media policy and use. What needs to be reinstated are public-interest arguments about cultural standards of quality in the media. These arguments take the form of promoting standards of intrinsic educational, scientific, aesthetic and artistic merit so as to draw out the 'best self' of the individual; and ensuring effective citizenship by regulating in the interests of media diversity, access, and the avoidance of negative stereotyping (on grounds of, for instance, race or gender).

Media studies needs to be more concerned with the question of *what* cultural standards need to be promoted and protected in the age of new media. The choice of this question by no means implies an abandonment of sociological insights or denigration of what sociology has to offer. Nor does it entail an unqualified commitment to philosophical idealism and a denial that there is a connection between aspects of cultural preference and socio-economic class position. What is involved is a rejection of the view that arguments about cultural standards can be simply reduced to class interest, notably the dominant ideology thesis, or to analysis (and celebration) of viewing as a process of negotiation between the text and its variously socially situated readers. There is a crucial component of the debate about cultural standards that has nothing to do with particular historical constellations of economic interest and social experience. It has to do with the characteristics of the texts themselves and how they are read, and not just in a narrow technical sense but, above all, in aesthetic and ethical senses.

In subjecting cultural discourse to its withering analysis, showing how the primacy of certain standards is rooted in the victory of one social vision over others, sociological scholars may believe that they have laid bare the myths of this discourse, exposing the insubstantiality of its standards and consigning them to oblivion. But without standards there would be no culture worth talking about, only sociology, and you cannot make cultural products with sociology. Cultural standards have a capacity to reconstitute themselves in changing social and historical contexts. That capacity has to be protected from those who would relativize culture to death as well as those who would reduce it to commodities like any other.

The economic significance of the 'cultural industries'

If the intellectual evolution of media studies has served to discredit the notion of cultural standards rooted in an ethics and an aesthetics that is not simply socially and historically conditioned, developments within the media and the arts world have played their own part. The key symptom of this change was the new currency gained by the concept of the 'cultural industries' by the 1980s. This concept drew attention to culture as a material process of the production and distribution of symbolic meanings, sharing features with other sectors of the economy.[38] In the process the connection between culture and the creative artist and between culture and the state was severed in favour of the assimilation of culture into the market economy. Emphasis in definitions of culture shifted to the arts as marketable commodities, and to the economic significance of the arts, for instance for employment and as a catalyst for other economic developments (for instance, in generating tourist-related employment and inner-city development).[39] Culture was 'sieved through the narrow accountancy of a sterile search for value for money'.[40] In the process the price of culture was allowed to obscure its value. The commitment to 'money for values' ceded place to 'value for money'.

It was not just a matter of culture falling into the expanding framework of professional economic analysis. The very particular moral agenda of liberalism, of privileging the individual over the community, extended its influence on the debate about culture. The imperialism of professional economics was the handmaiden of the hegemony of liberalism. This narrow ideology forcibly evicted debate about cultural standards in favour of the privileging of individual taste. With it came an anti-élite radicalism that strangely echoed positions in sociological media studies, albeit from a very contrasting ideological position. In the words of Rupert Murdoch, the international media tycoon:

> Much of what passes for quality on British television really is no more than a reflection of the values of a narrow elite which controls it and which has always thought its tastes are synonymous with quality – a view, incidentally, that is natural to all governing classes.[41]

As the media sociologist would be quick to establish, the concept of 'cultural industries' was supported by a range of media professionals seeking work opportunities and career advancement by means of the expansion of the media as an economic institution: advertisers, accountants, market researchers, public relations specialists, corporate planners. By redefinition of the media as institutions in a market economy they were offered scope to reshape the structures and practices of the 'industry' in their own image: by instituting 'internal markets', 'cost centres' and 'corporate strategies'. The result was new tensions and conflicts between creative artists and these newly confident media professionals and difficult dilemmas for the creative artist about whether and, if so, how to adapt to this changed working context. As one British television producer, Janet Street-Porter, put it in her address to the Edinburgh Television Festival in 1995, 'Television executives have been captured lemming-like by the language and mentality of the management consultant'.[42]

The technological changes linked to the new age of multimedia – and described as the 'digital revolution' – gave an even more central role to the 'cultural industries' in the emerging 'information' economy than could have been imagined when the term 'cultural industries' first came into use. Gurus like Nicholas Negroponte point to a limitless horizon of media possibilities over which the individual consumer will be sovereign.[43] He/she will be able to devise their own programmes; to construct their own viewing schedule; to interrogate information/text sources immediately; to use 'hypertext' to seek out more detailed materials; and to 'surf' at leisure on the Internet. In brief, 'the audience is me'. Driven in this case by the 'clever' computer and not limited by the 'dumb' television, the multimedia age promised to assimilate media, and therefore culture, into the parameters of the 'information' economy. Communication was being liberated from the constraints imposed by older technologies of transmission. This points to the future growth sector as not transmission technologies (which will be refined) but the provision of content for the new medium.

The problems with this type of analysis are that it confuses the highly plausible argument that technology reshapes culture, contains its own conditioning ideas and redistributes benefits and costs with the notion that culture – the content of a medium – is simply relative to that technology. Like the sociological conception of culture that prevails within media studies, the economic conception that excites many media professionals is essentially relativist and narrow in its view of quality – in this case celebrating individual taste as the source of cultural standards. In fact, the formula 'the audience is me' puts the issues of the ethics and aesthetics of media use at the heart of the problem of responsibility in the media in a new way (see the chapters by Dyson, Lübbe and Schulze). Also, issues of selection and shaping of material by editors and publishers, the very essence of quality control, will remain important as programme producers seek to establish 'brand' products in the new market (making the ethics and aesthetics of media production of enduring significance, as Hoffmann-Riem and Winterhoff-Spurk stress). But the visionaries of the multimedia information economy tend to evade or marginalize such issues. Criteria of ethical judgement and aesthetic judgement transcend the specificities of economics and technology as well as of social change. Cultures may be reconstituted by economic, technological and social changes. But that factor does not make the economist, the technologist or the sociologist the appropriate person to advise the media about cultural standards; and without such standards there would be no culture worth speaking about.

Conclusion

To argue for the continuing relevance of Matthew Arnold's ideas may seem oddly, even bizarrely, anachronistic. There are clearly serious problems in seeking to transpose modes of cultural criticism from one technological age (Arnold's print-centred culture) to another (the digital age). As Postman argues in this volume, every technology has its own philosophy and makes war against the philosophy embedded in old technology. Moreover, its effects are ecological. Hence, as sociologists would emphasize, the world of Arnold is not the world of television or multimedia. But the basic questions remain the same: what kind of media we construct; and how we choose to use those media. These questions return us to the same aesthetic and ethical issues that so deeply troubled Arnold and that should preoccupy us – but are so neglected in contemporary media studies and by the professional groups that are immediately benefiting from new technology (like the marketing specialists, advertisers and accountants).

Clearly, we cannot apply Arnold's strictures without reference to a vastly changed and changing technological and social context of media. As Homolka points out, typographic culture can be said to have reached its high point at about the time that Arnold was writing. Arnold's language was suffused with its modes of thought. Now the technological context appears to be radically altered by electronics and the digital revolution, bringing with it what Baudrillard refers to as the era of the code (the digital code). Take the example of television. Television values imagery and immediacy. It is a medium of ephemeral and literal images, very culturally heterogeneous in its products (from classic dramas and documentaries to soap operas and quiz shows), relatively low in its symbolic density, and reliant on its 'friendliness'/sociability and a rhythm of frequent 'high spots' and exclamatory styles of presentation to hold audiences.[44] These features involve a bias towards quick emotional responses and immediate gratification. They foster a limited attention span. Moreover, television's aesthetics are dispersed across a variety of genres (like news, documentaries, classic dramas, soap operas, quiz shows), involving differences of subject matter, content, form, style and materials. This heterogeneity appears to make judgements of quality problematic. And, in addition, judgements of quality need to distinguish between programme (where formal aesthetic criteria are most important) and schedule (where ethical issues about balance, variety and audience appeal become most prominent). Against this technological and commercial background, and its implications for television culture, and even more so as a new age of 'multimedia' takes over, it is perhaps not surprising that media studies has hesitated to take on board the quality issue.[45] But it does not follow from the fact that judgements of quality are problematic in relation to the electronic media that they cannot be made; that we are incapable of living outside the reach of the code being established by information technology. Nor does it follow that the idea of quality television is an oxymoron.

With 'multimedia' the profound ethical and aesthetic challenge comes from the new burden of responsibility that lies with the individual once the constraints on communications are so radically eased, if not eliminated. Schulze and Lübbe point out the implications in their chapters. Yet, in the face of so dramatic a technological change, we need also a sense of what remains enduring. Herein lies the importance of Homolka's chapter. The computer-based multimedia offer a new means of encoding written language and the modification of text by hypertext and the combination of text with moving images and sound. At the same time the printed word is different in character from other media, simply because language is its material – with its familiar meanings, rhythms and sonorities – and because the form of language is closest to being our form of life. Intellectually and aesthetically, as Dyson and Homolka stress, nothing can replace – or match – the literary arts and the activity of reading. In so far as television 'culture' and computer 'culture' demote the literary arts and the practice of critical reading they represent an assault on quality. The simultaneous decline of narrative fiction books and the rise of television soap operas and quiz shows and of computer games are testament to the way in which the commercial forces of consumerism have appealed to our 'ordinary selves' over our 'better selves', reducing our capacity for sustained aesthetic and intellectual engagement.

We are mistaken if we believe that the issues that so concerned Arnold are no longer relevant and that he can be dismissed as simply the prisoner of an old-fashioned conservative ideology of control or the representative of a redundant world of technology and media. Those issues relate to Arnold's sense of social and moral purpose, based on re-establishing the enduring significance of the distinction between our 'ordinary selves' and our 'better selves'. The cultural project of a citizenry that is not just basically literate but, above all, critically literate has lost none of its relevance, as the chapters by Dyson and Homolka argue. It is about developing and sustaining a particular value system: 'a way of thinking and feeling about the possibilities of a better life'.[46] Similarly, following the argument in Hoffmann-Riem's chapter, the political/constitutional project of guaranteeing the rights of the viewer/media user as a citizen remains as vital as ever.

But these cultural and constitutional projects are not addressed by simply celebrating 'popular culture' postmodernist-style, by the 'faith in machinery' of the apostles of 'multimedia', or by promoting the commercial potential of the 'cultural industries'. The 'cultural industries', 'multimedia' and 'popular culture' are powerful dimensions – indeed constitutive elements – of modern media and their development. Their promoters do not, however, address the ethical and aesthetic issues and arguments and certainly cannot provide an appropriate response to them. The debate about the age of new media offers little evidence that skills of discrimination – ethical and aesthetic – are being more effectively promoted and disseminated by 'men of culture' or that 'a stream of fresh thought' is being turned upon 'our stock notions and habits'. It seems rather to illustrate the point that, though human beings may have the potential to discriminate between good and bad, right and wrong, they also have an extraordinarily fertile ability to evade or fudge such choices.

References

1. M. Arnold, *Culture and Anarchy*, London: Smith Elder, 1869.
2. Arnold, *Culture and Anarchy*, pp. 12–13.
3. Arnold, *Culture and Anarchy*, p. 17.
4. M. Arnold, *Essays in Criticism*, 2nd series, London: Macmillan, 1915 edn, p. 2.

5. For instance in the United States see H. Bloom, *The Western Canon*, London: Macmillan, 1994; and in Britain see R. Hoggart, 'Why treat us like dimwits?', *Independent on Sunday*, 19 February 1995, p. 21 and, borrowing his title from Trollope, *The Way We Live Now*, forthcoming, 1996.

6. Respective examples might be P. Bourdieu, 'The aristocracy of culture', *Media, Culture and Society* 2 (1980), pp. 225–54; J. Fiske, *Television Culture*, London: Routledge, 1987; and J.-F. Lyotard, *La Condition postmoderne: rapport sur le savoir*, Paris: Minuit, 1979.

7. *Report of the Committee on Broadcasting 1960*, Cmnd 1753, London: HMSO, 1962.

8. D. Strinati, *An Introduction to Theories of Popular Culture*, London: Routledge, 1995, p. 42.

9. On the social function of aesthetics see P. Bourdieu, 'Outline of a sociological theory of art perception', *International Social Sciences Journal* 2 (1968), pp. 225–54. Also P. Bourdieu, *Distinction: A Social Critique of the Judgement of Taste*, London: Routledge, 1986.

10. For the propaganda model of mass media see E. Herman and N. Chomsky, *Manufacturing Consent: The Political Economy of Mass Media*, London: Vantage, 1994.

11. J. Storey, *An Introductory Guide to Cultural Theory and Popular Culture*, London: Harvester Wheatsheaf, 1993.

12. S. Hall, 'The rediscovery of ideology: the return of the repressed' in M. Gurevitch, T. Bennett, J. Curran and J. Woollacott (eds), *Culture, Society and the Media*, London: Methuen, 1982.

13. H. Marcuse, *One-Dimensional Man*, London: Sphere, 1968.

14. T. Adorno, *The Culture Industry: Selected Essays on Mass Culture*, London: Routledge, 1991.

15. T. Adorno, *Aesthetic Theory*, trans. C. Lenhardt, London: Routledge, 1984.

16. W. Benjamin, 'The work of art in the age of mechanical reproduction', reprinted in his *Illuminations*, Glasgow: Fontana, 1973.

17. Classically, the work of the Swiss linguist Saussure, the French social anthropologist Lévi-Strauss and, more recently, in literary criticism Umberto Eco. For the semiological study of popular culture see R. Barthes, *Mythologies*, London: Paladin, 1973. More generally, see J. Culler, *Structuralist Poetics*, London: Routledge & Kegan Paul, 1975.

18. For critiques of structuralism see J. Corner, 'Codes and cultural analysis', *Media, Culture and Society* 2 (1980), pp. 73–86; and J. Merquior, *From Prague to Paris*, London: Verso, 1986.

19. M. Foucault, *Power/Knowledge: Selected Interviews and Other Writings 1972–1977*, ed. C. Gordon, New York: Harvester Wheatsheaf, 1980. For examples in media studies see N. Fairclough, *Media Discourse*, London: Edward Arnold, 1995 and M. Macdonald, *Myths of Femininity in the Popular Media*, London: Edward Arnold, 1995.

20. I. Ang, *Desperately Seeking the Audience*, London: Routledge, 1991.
21. S. Fish, *Is There a Text in This Class? The Authority of Interpretive Communities*, Cambridge, MA: Harvard University Press, 1980.
22. J. Baudrillard, *Selected Writings*, ed. M. Poster, Stanford, CA: Stanford University Press, 1988.
23. M. de Certeau, *The Practice of Everyday Life*, Berkeley, CA: University of California Press, 1984. Also H. Jenkins, *Textual Poachers: Television Fans and Participatory Culture*, London: Routledge, 1992. For general overviews of postmodernism see N. Denzin, *Images of Postmodern Society: Social Theory and Contemporary Cinema*, London: Sage, 1991; A. McRobbie, *Postmodernism and Popular Culture*, London: Routledge, 1994; P. Waugh, *Practising Postmodernism/Reading Modernism*, London: Edward Arnold, 1992; and P. Waugh (ed.), *Postmodernism: A Reader*, London: Edward Arnold, 1992.
24. M. Featherstone, *Consumer Culture and Postmodernism*, London: Sage, 1991.
25. Z. Bauman, *Intimations of Postmodernity*, London: Routledge, 1992 and *Postmodern Ethics*, Oxford: Oxford University Press, 1993. More generally, see H. Bertens, *The Idea of the Postmodern*, London: Routledge, 1995.
26. See M. Foucault, *The History of Sexuality*, Harmondsworth: Penguin, 1978 and R. Barthes, *The Pleasures of the Text*, New York: Hill & Wang, 1975.
27. Denzin, *Images of Postmodern Society*; Fiske, *Television Culture*.
28. Fish, *Is There a Text in This Class?*; J.-F. Lyotard, 'Complexity and the sublime' in L. Appignanesi (ed.), *Postmodernism: ICA Documents 5*, London: ICA, 1986.
29. On the concept of cultural capital see P. Bourdieu, *Distinction: A Social Critique of the Judgment of Taste*; also his *The Field of Cultural Production: Essays on Art and Literature*, Cambridge: Polity Press, 1993.
30. Classically, see R. Williams, 'Culture is ordinary' in N. McKenzie (ed.), *Convictions*, London: MacGibbon & Kee, 1958.
31. For an overview see chs 10, 12 and 14 of Fiske, *Television Culture*.
32. For an overview of such work see A. Gray and J. McGuigan (eds), *Studying Culture: An Introductory Reader*, London: Edward Arnold, 1993. Also Strinati, *An Introduction to Theories of Popular Culture*.
33. R. Barthes, *The Pleasure of the Text*.
34. S. Hall, 'Encoding/decoding' in S. Hall, D. Hobson, A. Lowe and P. Willis (eds), *Culture, Media, Language*, London: Hutchinson, 1980, pp. 128–39; Fiske, *Television Culture*. For a critique of Fiske see G. Murdock, 'Cultural Studies at the crossroads', *Australian Journal of Communication* 16 (1989).
35. J. Fiske, *Understanding Popular Culture*, London: Unwin Hyman, 1989, p. 47.

36. R. Hoggart, *The Way We Live Now*, forthcoming, 1996; J. McGuigan, *Cultural Populism*, London: Routledge, 1992 on the 'uncritical populist drift' in cultural studies; T. Gitlin, 'The politics of communication and the communication of politics' in J. Curran and M. Gurevitch (eds), *Mass Media and Society*, London: Edward Arnold, 1991, pp. 329–41; M. Morris, 'Banality in cultural studies', *Block* 14 (1988); and G. Murdock and P. Golding, 'Information poverty and political inequality: citizenship in the age of privatized communication', *Journal of Communication*, 1989.

37. J. Baudrillard, *Baudrillard Live: Selected Interviews*, ed. M. Gane, London: Routledge, 1993.

38. N. Garnham, 'Concepts of culture – public policy and the cultural industries' in Gray and McGuigan (eds), *Studying Culture*, pp. 54–61 (first published in 1983).

39. See Arts Council of Great Britain, *A Great British Success Story*, London, 1985; Arts Council, *Partnership: Making Arts Money Work Harder*, London, 1986; and J. Myerscough, *The Economic Importance of the Arts*, London: Policy Studies Institute, 1988.

40. R. Hewison, *Culture and Consensus: England, Art and Politics Since 1940*, London: Methuen, 1995.

41. R. Murdoch, McTaggart Lecture delivered at the Edinburgh International Festival, 25 August 1989.

42. A classic example of these tensions and conflicts is provided by the BBC under John Birt, noticeably the attacks by Andrew Davies, Janet Street-Porter, Dennis Potter and John Tusa in 1994–95 on a management which was resorting to 'formula' drama and a 'grim efficiency' at the expense of journalistic effectiveness and for which the notion of 'objectives' was replacing that of 'ideas'.

43. N. Negroponte, *Being Digital*, London: Hodder & Stoughton, 1995.

44. Nicely summarized in J. Corner, *Television Form and Public Address*, London: Edward Arnold, 1995, pp. 168–72.

45. A major exception has been work by the British Film Institute. See G. Mulgan (ed.), *Questions of Quality*, London: British Film Institute, 1990. Note also G. Brandt (ed.), *British Television Drama*, Cambridge: Cambridge University Press, 1993. More recently, the issue of quality has been taken up in D. McQuail, *Media Performance: Mass Communication and the Public Interest*, London: Sage, 1992, and in Corner, *Television Form and Public Address*.

46. Hewison, *Culture and Consensus*.

2

Defending Ourselves Against the Seductions of Eloquence

NEIL POSTMAN

The title of this chapter – 'Defending ourselves against the seductions of eloquence' – comes from some remarks made by Bertrand Russell in discussing the purpose of education. In using the phrase 'the seductions of eloquence', Russell was talking about talking, that is to say, language, and how it is necessary to help the young resist being seduced by its mysterious charms. Not surprisingly, and as Russell was well aware, we actually know something about how to do that, and have been working on the problem for at least 2,500 years. The curriculum known as the trivium, invented by the Greeks, consisted of the study of logic, rhetoric and grammar, and one of its purposes was to assist the young in distancing themselves from language so that they would not be entirely within its thrall. I might say, in passing, that we need to work on this problem since there is ample evidence that language, in all of its forms, is still used successfully by some people to make fools of the rest of us. Indeed, many of us use our own language to seduce ourselves into foolishness and sometimes dangerous foolishness. But my focus is not on language but on technology, about which most people know very little, and which has almost as much power as does language to seduce us by its wonders into a kind of sleepy stupidity.

So what I propose to do is outline six ideas about technology that, were they known to our young, would help them to defend themselves against the seductions of technological eloquence, that is to say, defend themselves against a dangerously naïve enthusiasm for new and alluring technologies that threaten to engulf them. I do not claim that these ideas are all that one needs to know. But I do claim that they represent the rudiments of understanding the role of technology in human affairs.

The cultural price of technology

The first idea is that all technological change is a Faustian bargain. This means that for every advantage a new technology offers, there is always a corresponding disadvantage. The disadvantage may exceed in importance the advantage, or the advantage may well be worth the cost. Now, this may seem to be a rather obvious idea, but you would be surprised at how many people believe that new technologies are unmixed blessings. You need only think of the enthusiasm with which most people approach their understanding of computers. Ask anyone who knows something about computers to talk about them, and you will find that they will, unabashedly and relentlessly, extol the wonders of computers. You will also find that in most cases they will completely neglect to mention any of the disadvantages of computers. This is a dangerous imbalance, since the greater the wonders of a technology, the greater will be its negative consequences. Think of the automobile, which, for all its obvious advantages, has poisoned our air, choked our cities and degraded the beauty of our natural landscape. Or you might reflect on the paradox of medical technology, which brings wondrous cures but is, at the same time, a demonstrable cause of disease and disability, and has played a significant role in reducing the diagnostic skills of physicians.

It is also well to recall that, for all the intellectual and social benefits provided by the printing press, its costs were actually monumental. The printing press gave the Western world prose, but it made poetry into an exotic and elitist form of communication. It gave us inductive science, but it reduced religious sensibility to a form of fanciful superstition. Printing gave us the modern conception of nationhood, but in so doing turned patriotism into a sordid if not lethal emotion. We might even say that the printing of the Bible in vernacular languages introduced the impression that God was an Englishman or a German or a Frenchman – that is to say, printing reduced God to the dimensions of a local potentate.

Perhaps the best way I can express this idea is to say that the question 'What will a new technology do?' is no more important than the question 'What will a new technology *undo*?' Indeed, the latter question is more important, precisely because it is asked so infrequently. One might say, then, that those with a mature perspective on technology are people who are capable of doing some technological cost-accounting, people who know that technology giveth and technology taketh away, people who are at all times sceptical of utopian and Messianic visions drawn by those who have no sense of history or of the precarious balances on which culture depends.

Who benefits?

Idea number one, then, is that culture always pays a price for technology. This leads to the second idea, which is that the advantages and disadvantages of new technologies are never distributed evenly among the population. This means that every new technology benefits some and harms others. There are even some who are not affected at all. Consider again the case of the printing press in the sixteenth century. By placing the word of God on every Christian's kitchen table, the mass-produced book undermined the authority of the church hierarchy, and hastened the break-up of the Holy Roman See. Since some of you are Protestants, had you lived in that period, you would have cheered this development. The Catholics among you would have been enraged and distraught. As a Jew, I couldn't have given a damn one way or another, since it would make no difference whether a pogrom was inspired by Martin Luther or Pope Leo X. Some gain, some lose, a few remain as they were.

Let us take another example, television, although here I should add at once that in the case of television there are very few indeed who are not affected in one way or another. In America, where television has taken hold more deeply than anywhere else, there are many people who find it a blessing, not least those who have achieved high-paying, gratifying careers in television as executives, technicians, directors, newscasters and entertainers. On the other hand, and in the long run, television may bring to an end the careers of schoolteachers since school was an invention of the printing press and must stand or fall on the issue of how much importance the printed word will have in the future. There is no chance, of course, that television will go away but schoolteachers who are enthusiastic about its presence always call to my mind an image of some turn-of-the-century blacksmith who not only sings the praises of the automobile but who also believes that his business will be enhanced by it. We now know that his business was not enhanced by it; it was rendered obsolete by it, as perhaps an intelligent blacksmith would have known.

The questions, then, that are never far from the mind of a person who is knowledgeable about technological change are these: who specifically benefits from the development of a new technology? which groups, what type of person, what kind of industry will be favoured, and, of course, which groups of people will thereby be harmed?

These questions should certainly be on our minds when we think about computer technology. There is no doubt that the computer has been and will continue to be advantageous to large-scale organizations like the Pentagon or airline companies or banks or tax collecting institutions. And it is equally clear that the computer is now indispensable to high-level researchers in physics and other natural sciences. But to what extent has computer technology been an advantage to the masses of people? To steel workers, vegetable store owners, automobile mechanics, musicians, bakers, bricklayers, dentists and most of the rest into whose lives the computer now intrudes? These people have had their private affairs made more accessible to powerful institutions. They are more easily tracked and controlled; they are subjected to more examinations, and are increasingly mystified by the decisions made about them. They are more than ever reduced to mere numerical objects. They are being buried by junk mail. They are easy targets for advertising agencies and political institutions. The schools want to teach their children to operate computers at the expense of teaching things that it may be more valuable for children to know.

In a word, these people are losers in the great computer revolution. The winners, which include among others computer companies, multinational corporations and the state, will, of course, encourage the losers to be enthusiastic about computer technology. That is the way of winners, and so they tell the losers that with personal computers the average person can balance a financial account more neatly, keep better track of recipes, and make more logical shopping lists. They also tell them that computers will make it possible to vote at home, shop and bank at home, get all the information they wish at home, and thus make community life unnecessary. They tell them that their lives will be conducted more efficiently, discreetly neglecting to say from whose point of view or what might be the costs of such efficiency. That is why it is always necessary for us to ask of those who speak enthusiastically of the computer: Why do you do this? What interests do you represent?

To whom are you hoping to give power and freedom? From whom will you be withholding power and freedom?

Every technology has a philosophy

I do not mean to attribute unsavoury, let alone sinister motives to anyone. I say only that since technology favours some people and harms others these are questions that must always be asked. And that is the second idea. Here is the third: Embedded in every technology there is a powerful idea, sometimes two or three powerful ideas. These ideas are often hidden from our view because they are of a somewhat abstract nature. But this should not be taken to mean that they do not have practical consequences. Let me give you some examples of what I mean, beginning with one that even after 200 years is still largely unnoticed by educators. I refer to the seemingly harmless practice of assigning marks or grades to the answers students give in examinations. This procedure seems so natural to most of us that we can hardly think about its significance; we may even find it difficult to imagine that a number or letter is a tool, or, if you will, a technology; and that when we use it to judge some-one's behaviour, we have taken a momentous step. In point of fact, the first instance of grading students' papers occurred at Cambridge University in the year 1792 at the suggestion of a tutor named William Farish. He probably was not aware of what he was starting but the idea that a quantitative value could be assigned to human thoughts was a major step toward constructing a mathematical concept of reality. If a number can be given to the quality of a thought, then a number can be given to the qualities of mercy, love, hate, beauty, creativity, intelligence, even sanity itself.

When Galileo said that the language of nature is written in mathematics he did not mean to include human feeling or accom-plishment or insight. Perhaps he was wrong. Our psychologists, sociologists and educators seem to find it impossible to do their work without numbers. Now, I will not argue here that theirs is a good idea or a bad idea, only that it *is* an idea, with practical consequences. And a peculiar idea at that. To say that someone should be doing better work because he has an IQ of 134, or that someone is a seven point two on a sensitivity scale or that this woman's essay on the rise of capitalism is an A− and that woman's is a C+ would have sounded like gibberish to Galileo or Goethe or

Shakespeare or Thomas Jefferson. If it makes sense to us, that is because our minds have been conditioned by the technology of numbers, so that we see the world differently from them. Again, I do not say better. I do not say worse. I say differently, which is what I mean when I say that embedded in every technology is an idea; that is, a way of seeing, talking about and valuing what is in the world.

Perhaps you are familiar with the old adage that says: to a man with a hammer, everything looks like a nail. We may extend that truism: to a person with a pencil, everything looks like a list. To a person with a television camera, everything looks like an image. To a person with a computer, everything looks like data. I do not think we need to take these aphorisms literally. But what they call to our attention is that every technology has a prejudice. Like language itself, it predisposes us to favour and value certain perspectives and accomplishments. In a culture without writing, human memory is of the greatest importance, as are the proverbs, sayings and songs which contain the accumulated oral wisdom of centuries. That is why Solomon was thought to be the wisest of men. In 1 Kings we are told he knew 3,000 proverbs. But in a culture *with* writing, such feats of memory are considered a waste of time, and proverbs are merely irrelevant fancies. The writing person favours logical organization and systematic analysis, not proverbs. The telegraphic person values speed, not introspection. The television person values immediacy, not history. And computer people, what shall we say of them? Perhaps we can say, as does Professor Joseph Weizenbaum of MIT, that the computer person values calculation, not judgement.

The third idea, then, is that every technology has a philosophy which is given expression in how the technology makes people use their minds, in what it makes us do with our bodies, in how it codifies the world, in which of our senses it amplifies, in which of our emotional and intellectual tendencies it disregards. This idea is the sum and substance of what Marshall McLuhan meant when he coined the famous sentence: 'The medium is the message.'

Media wars

Here is the fourth idea: The philosophy embedded in a new technology always makes war against the philosophy embedded in an old technology. Media compete with each other for time, for attention, for money, for prestige, and, above all, for the dominance of their world view. In the United States, such media wars can be seen everywhere – in politics, in religion, in commerce – but we see them most clearly in the schools where two great technologies confront each other for control of students' minds. On the one hand, there is the world of the printed word, with its emphasis on logic, sequence, history, exposition, objectivity and discipline. On the other, there is the world of television, with its emphasis on imagery, narrative, presentness, simultaneity, immediate gratification and emotional response. Our children come to school having been deeply conditioned by the biases of television. There, they encounter the biases of the printed word. A sort of psychic battle takes place, and there are many casualties: children who can't learn to read or won't, children who cannot organize into logical structures even a simple essay, children who cannot attend to lectures or explanations for more than five minutes at a time. They are failures, but not because they are stupid. They are failures because there is a media war going on, and they are on the wrong side – at least for the moment. Who knows what schools will be like 25 years from now? Or 50? The type of student who is currently a failure may be considered a success. The type who is now successful may be regarded as a handicapped learner.

To take another example: in introducing the personal computer to the classroom, we shall be breaking the truce of a 400-year-old media war between the gregariousness and openness of the oral tradition and the introspection and isolation of the printed word. Orality stresses group learning, co-operation and a sense of social responsibility. Print stresses individualized learning, competition and personal autonomy. Over four centuries, teachers have achieved a kind of pedagogical balance between these two orientations. So what is valuable in each can be maximized. Now comes the computer carrying anew the banner of private learning and individual problem-solving. Will the widespread use of computers in the classroom defeat once and for all the claims of communal speech? Will the computer raise egocentrism to the status of a virtue? I only raise the questions. I do not offer any answers. I say only that there is vitality and health in a balanced media environment, and one must always be concerned when that balance is threatened.

The ecological nature of technological change

The fifth idea is that technological change is not additive; it is ecological. I can explain this best by an analogy. What happens if we place a drop of red dye into a beaker of clear water? Do we now have clear water plus a spot of red dye? Obviously not. We have a new coloration to every molecule of water. That is what I mean by ecological change. A new medium does not add something; it changes everything. In the year 1500, after the printing press was invented, you did not have old Europe plus the printing press. You had a different Europe. After television, America was not America plus television. Television gave a new coloration to every political campaign, to every home, to every school, to every church, to every industry, and so on.

That is why we must be cautious about technological innovation. The consequences of technological change are always vast, often unpredictable and largely irreversible. That is also why it is reasonable to be suspicious of capitalists. Capitalists are by definition not only personal risk takers but, more to the point, cultural risk takers. The most creative and daring of them hope to exploit new technologies to the fullest, and do not much care what traditions are overthrown in the process or whether or not a culture is prepared to function without such traditions. Capitalists are, in a word, radicals. In America, our most significant radicals have always been capitalists – men like Bell, Edison, Ford, Carnegie, Sarnoff, Goldwyn. These men obliterated the nineteenth century, and created the twentieth, which is why it is a mystery to me that capitalists are thought to be conservative. Perhaps it is because they are inclined to wear dark suits and grey ties.

I trust you understand that in saying all this, I am making no argument for socialism. I say only that entrepreneurs are in no sense conservatives. They need to be carefully watched and disciplined. They talk of family, marriage, piety, and honour, but if they are allowed to exploit technology to its fullest economic potential, they invariably undo the institutions that make such ideas possible. And here I might give two examples of this point, taken from the American encounter with technology. First, from politics. It is clear by now that the people who have had the most radical effect on American politics in our time are not political ideologues or student protesters with long hair and copies of Karl Marx under their arms.

The radicals who have changed the nature of politics in America are entrepreneurs in dark suits and grey ties who manage the large television industry in America. They did not mean to turn political discourse into a form of entertainment. They did not mean to make it impossible for an overweight person to run for high political office. They did not mean to reduce political campaigning to a 30-second television commercial. All they were trying to do was to make television into a vast and unsleeping money machine. That they destroyed substantive political discourse in the process does not concern them.

Similarly, we might say that the people who have had the most profound effect on American education in this century are not philosophers, teachers or social critics. The radicals who have changed American education are quiet entrepreneurs who live in an affluent suburban town called Princeton, New Jersey. There they developed and marketed the technology known as the standardized test, most especially the notorious Scholastic Aptitude Test. Teachers all over America have been required to teach to that test so that their students can achieve good scores. To put it plainly, the test controls the curriculum, and that is as good an example of the tyranny of technology as I know.

Domesticating technology

I turn now to the final idea. Up to now, I have been using the words 'technology' and 'medium' interchangeably, as is commonly done. But I think it useful to make a distinction between them, in the following way: A technology is to a medium as the brain is to the mind. Like the brain, a technology is merely an instrument, a piece of hard wiring, so to speak. Like the mind, a medium is a *use* to which we put the instrument. This does not mean that either the brain or technology can be put to *any* use we see fit. There is a structure to our brains which limits what we can do with them. And the same is true of technologies. If you invent a 747 jet plane, you *will* not and indeed cannot use it to carry commuters from Mainz to Frankfurt. If you invent television, you can, but probably will not, use it merely to display words on a screen, in the manner of a printed page. If you invent a computer you are probably making a serious mistake if you use it merely as an electronic workbook. Technologies, like our brains, *want* to be used in certain ways, frequently *demand* to be used in certain ways. But this does not mean that these ways are always clear or that we have nothing to say in the matter. To some extent, we can make a technology into a medium that consciously serves our best interests rather than unconsciously opposes them. Here, the issue becomes very complicated because in its transformation to a medium, a technology is always shaped by the social, political and economic systems into which it is introduced. The uses to which we in America put television are not the same as in China or Russia, in part because each of us has different traditions, different media environments and different economic systems.

But the main point is that we *are* not, and should not think of ourselves as, helpless in the face of technology. A technology is dangerous only to the extent that we abdicate our responsibility for its control. In contemplating a new technology, I have always found it extremely useful to pose the question 'What is the troublesome problem to which this technology is the solution?' Assuming there is a problem – and quite often there is not – I find it useful to ask, further, 'In solving this problem, what new problems will the technology create?' Such questions, if commonly asked, begin the process of domesticating technology, of making technologies into benign media, of making technology behave itself in the way we try to make our brain behave itself.

Conclusion

I shall proceed to do just that with my own brain by moving toward a close. But first, with your indulgence, I should like to summarize the six ideas. First, culture always pays a price for technology – the greater the technology, the greater the price; second, the assets and liabilities of technology are not evenly distributed, and the winners always try to persuade the losers that they are really winners; third, every technology has its unique view of the world, which is sometimes an advantage and sometimes not; fourth, technologies compete with each other for dominance; fifth, technological change is ecological, not additive; and, sixth, the distinction between a technology and a medium provides us with an opportunity to control social change.

Now, as I said at the start, I do not claim that these ideas are the only ideas we need to know. But they are, I believe, sound generalizations about the interaction of culture and technology; and in closing, I am prepared to say this of them. In America and Europe, we have paid little attention to such ideas, and that is because in the West we love our technology more than we respect our history or our traditions or our children or our political system. And as you know, when people are in love, they see no faults in their beloved, spend most of their time singing the praises of their beloved, are willing to sacrifice everything for the sake of their beloved, and, as a result, know nothing whatever *about* their beloved. I assume all of us wish to proceed more intelligently, for the sake of our children, if for nothing else.

Note

This chapter was originally published as 'Selbstverteidigung gegen die Lockungen der technologischen Beredsamkeit' in H. Hoffmann (ed.), *Gestern begann die Zukunft*, Darmstadt: Wissenschaftliche Buchgesellschaft, 1994, pp. 17–26.

3

On the Threshold of a New Era in Media History: What Follows the Period of Technological Innovation?

GERHARD SCHULZE

We would all be surely forgiven for questioning the sanity of a person who, having just eaten an enormous meal at home, took herself/himself off to a restaurant and ordered fish and chips thirty times. In the same way, one must ask whether the same sort of judgement is deserved by the emerging period in media history, offering as it does an aimless and endless journey into the new world of multimedia. We are already confronted by a grotesque over-supply of media. By what devil are we driven to order many times more television and computer-based programmes?

Of course, this comparison is not wholly satisfying. What is clear is that we are facing a massive digestive problem. But it is not we ourselves, the consumers, who are serving up this nightmare land of milk and honey, like children who overfill their plates. Our only means of action as media consumers is the personal decision to decline what is on offer. More organized and effective forms of resistance are denied to us. We must also absolve from blame those traditional scapegoats of the cultural critic, the corporate actors in the media industry and the organized interests in the political system. It would be naïve to demand that the economic and political activists behind the development of new media should cease their activities. Such a demand could not be expected to produce any practical effect. There are good reasons why the critical approaches to media policy that dominated the 1960s and 1970s have gradually lost ground. There is little real substance, for instance, in the myth of the innocent consumer manipulated by evil men in the media companies and the political parties (see Winterhoff-Spurk's chapter). The viewer cannot be absolved of all blame. Nor can blame be heaped solely on the media and political institutions,

where many would have preferred nothing better than to retain the
status quo.

Even if the forthcoming turbulences in the media market are to
some extent the product of human action, they remain beyond the
realm of moral judgement like the weather. The new information
and communications technologies are simply overwhelming us.
The attempt to reflect on whether we ought to improve particular
regulatory arrangements and market structures is a waste of time.
What remains for us as the central challenge is a process of intellectual preparation for the time *after* the new media opportunities
created by technology are in place. What will we do then? This is
the central question with which this chapter is concerned.

Reflecting about the future

But first we must confront the criticism that it may not make any
sense to put this question. As Hans Jonas stated in one of his last
interviews, 'Anyone who believes that he is able to predict the
future is from the outset not to be taken seriously'. And yet Jonas
was precisely the kind of philosopher who sought to reflect about
the future. There are, of course, different forms of concern with
tomorrow's world: those that are ridiculous and those that are to be
taken seriously.

What is ridiculous is a form of prognosis in which society is
conceived as being like a piece of clockwork. Apparently one needs
only to programme a computer to replicate how society functions.
In this category of thinking about the future belong the many
reports that dress up trend extrapolations in scientific language and
establish their competence by a mystique of quantification – with
a small allowance for margin of error, and a great willingness
to forget what has been forecast as soon as it becomes clear that
everything has turned out quite differently.

The only form of reflection about the future to be taken seriously
is that which takes account of the essential openness of history. The
sensible questions are the following. If particular contextual changes
occur, who will then have to take on prime responsibility for
managing them? What will be the sensible course of action? And
what can one be doing now to prepare? With these questions in mind
this chapter explores its central theme – the nature and implications
of a new era in media history.

The argument that there is no future

But, before embarking on this task, we must return to the question of whether the theme itself can be sensibly addressed. The attack on naïvety is a recurring feature of the intellectual landscape of the 1990s. It is expressed in the form of the following book titles as translated from the German: *Ascent into Nothing* (Herbert Gruhl, 1992), *The Audacity of the Unsuspecting* (Jürgen Dahl, 1989) and *The End: On Our Merry Hopelessness in the Face of Ecological Catastrophe* (Gregory Fuller, 1993). Following these books, one might ask – why bother concerning ourselves about the future if there is no future for human beings? The anthropologist Richard Leakey, certainly a serious man, a scientist whom one cannot suspect of posing for effect, remembers at the end of his book *Origins* (1977) the five big mass exterminations which have already occurred in the history of the earth. He does so in order to point out the geo-historical 'normalcy' of the sixth mass extermination that is without doubt already under way. In Leakey's view man as a species will in all probability fall victim to this process.

I cannot embrace Leakey's view. What distinguishes the sixth mass extermination from the previous five is the cause. Whereas all previous mass exterminations had their origins in natural events, the cause of the sixth is clearly man himself. But man is capable of learning to deal with such situations and of continuously adapting himself. From an evolutionary perspective of history the information technology revolution provides just the type of quantum leap in the improvement of man's capacity for learning and adaptation that he needs for his survival.

One could, of course, object that, given the scale of the challenges, man's chances are not all that promising. But this type of futuristic argument is not to be taken too seriously. Why should one completely squander what is perhaps only a small chance of survival by having decided not to make use of it? *If*, however, one decides to make use of the chance, one must also think about the time *afterwards*. For what purpose ought one to attempt to save one's life, if by the success of this enterprise one would be thrown into such confusion and lack of a sense of meaning that one began to consider suicide? For the greatest requirement of the future, if there is to be one, could prove to be the problem of making something sensible out of one's life.

The coming period of technological innovation is the last

The next step in the development of media brings us a good deal nearer to a future in which, to a new degree, the central problem will be one of making something sensible out of one's life. Perhaps media history began with the notion of breaking off a branch of a tree with the object of letting others know that someone had been there. Since that time the historical path of development of media technology can be described by a single idea: that of breaking free, as far as is practically possible, from the constraints of face-to-face communication.

An overview of media history up to the present yields two basic conclusions. Firstly, every wave of technological innovation is only a milestone in a historical process, not an endpoint. And, secondly, technological changes unleash changes in cultural forms – the theme of Postman's chapter. The experience of the 1980s has once again confirmed the importance and relevance of these two conclusions.

However – and this point is central to the argument of this chapter – the accuracy of this model of media history will hold for only one more time and then never again. The emerging threshold of a new age in media history is of a special type – because it is the *last* of its type. For a last time in media history the engineers, product innovators and research and development staff will be once again able to break up cultural and social models that had begun to consolidate themselves. Beyond this impending level of media development no more such powerful shifts of technological frontiers will be possible, only small marginal adjustments without deep cultural effects.

The situation in media technology is in this respect not different from that in other product areas. At some point or other the scope for product development is used up. The product can provide all that even the most eccentric consumer might want from it. Indeed there is an increasing number of examples of products whose attributes go way beyond the likely needs of consumers.

'Unlimited' media

What this means in the case of media technology is taking on an ever clearer shape. What appeared yesterday to be still remote is already reality today: the multiplication of channels of communication; the perfecting of possibilities for interactive communication; convergence of television, video, telephone, fax and personal computers; the availability of new forms of direct subscription, as in the form of pay-television and pay-per-view video; development of 'virtual reality' experiences; radical globalization of media companies and media product manufacture and marketing; the construction of giant archives of films, games, texts, information, educational materials, available to all who can pay.

Today the dreamer appears to be the person who seeks to *exclude* anything that can be done by means of media technology. New examples are the 'virtual' psychotherapist or the use of virtual reality to book a hotel room after 'visiting' it and 'looking round' the rooms and facilities. Already daily life is being altered: home shopping, tele-banking, booking holidays by personal computer, seeking out partners on the Internet, videoconferences, interactive electronic teaching and learning, return to working from home, electronic books and newspapers, new video games, new experience parks with virtual worlds, development of specialist television channels ('narrowcasting'), activation of the viewer by possibilities for participation as for instance in the choice of camera angles or in deciding how a narrative develops.

The contemporary change in the media landscape is perhaps best described as its *final release from the constraints of limitation*. By 'unlimited' media is meant that the scope of possibilities available to the users of the media is growing way beyond the bounds of human capacities to make full use of these possibilities.

But all this exciting and theatrical activity on the stage of media diverts attention from the underlying fundamental fact: that media technology as a dominant actor in cultural history is disappearing from the centre stage into the wings. While media technology prepares itself once again powerfully to transform the world, it is already becoming clear that its role is being played out. The history of media up to the present was determined to a great extent by technological revolutions. Its future path will now only depend on what we do with that technology.

The 'post-technological' society

The process by which technology is creating 'unlimited' media is part of a more general expansion of opportunities in cultural history. A stage of human history is drawing nearer that might be characterized as 'post-technological'.

Much the most important feature of technological civilization is cognitive in nature. This civilization possesses an underlying sense of basic direction, of certainty, of a definite way in which man can progress. The market provides signals about what people want; the natural sciences clarify the question of the means by which these wishes can be realized; on the basis of this foundation of scientific knowledge engineers design systems and procedures; while firms produce the resulting goods and services and respond to new signals from the market.

Despite its power as a model, over a long period society has functioned to only a limited extent in this clockwork-like manner (bearing in mind that, like clockwork, it suffers from faults and stoppages). Yet our thinking remains completely trapped in the structure described above. There still appears to be enough evidence to support the idea that society functions in this mechanical way. Of course, the biggest challenge to this model of technological thought, the global ecological crisis, has only just begun.

Nevertheless, the path of technological civilization is finite, an illustration of which is the impending innovation shock in media technology. In the final analysis nothing more is left for technology to do than the tasks of maintenance and replacement of systems and products and the invention of minor modifications.

But when all that is technologically feasible is done: what then? This core question of the dawning 'post-technological' age might appear more appropriate for those who live in this future utopia. In fact, it has already secreted itself into the fabric of our daily lives. It is the question that confronts the holiday-maker, the shopper, the magazine buyer, the person suddenly confronted by an over-full wardrobe, the lover of music who has collected together more compact discs than he/she can ever listen to, the amateur photographer with the most modern equipment but no proper idea about how to use it, and the television viewer with a remote control in her/his hand. For a long time technology has offered us a multiplication of our capacity for consumption in many areas of our daily lives. For a long time we have been operating in a realm of possibilities that we can no longer assimilate, indeed that we can no longer even grasp in their totality.

The 'experience society': its practical implications as a philosophy for our daily lives

The philosophy of daily life identified here as that of the 'experience society' can be seen as the first attempt to provide a collective approach to tackling the problem of the world of 'unlimited' media. Since the end of the 1960s there has been a spread of an attitude to life that one might characterize as 'the rationality of experience'. Rationality refers to the pursuit of given ends with the optimal means and a continuous striving to improve the relation between ends and means. The 'rationality of experience' means to define the ends in the context of the subject. Such an approach to managing life involves arranging external conditions with the intention of achieving the best possible internal effects. The 'rationality of experience' is in essence the transference of the logic of controlling nature to the body and mind. One tackles one's self in the way that an engineer works on the improvement of a product, of say a vacuum-cleaner. Just as the engineer believes that he/she can increase the quality of the vacuum-cleaner by the intelligent application of her/his technical expertise, so the technician of experience hopes to approximate more closely to the goals of the good life by an intelligent arrangement of external conditions. The 'rationality of experience' encompasses everything: the world of material products, lifestyles, choice of partners, whether or not to have children, educational and career development routes, and, more than anything else, the way in which we deal with the media.

The malaise at the heart of the 'experience society'

What we cannot avoid noticing is a malaise at the heart of the 'experience society'. The argument that dozens or hundreds of goods or services on offer would better meet the needs of consumers than two or three seems only to make sense in terms of an infantile logic according to which happiness has been finally attained once it is no longer possible to put another piece of chocolate in one's mouth. Just how much truth there is in this philosophy becomes apparent when one considers the sad fate of the enthusiastic partisans of television in the 1960s and 1970s. They have evolved into a mass of 'zappers' who at best feel amused, but are mostly bored. They feel uncomfortable when confronted by the question of whether they are missing something better by just endlessly consuming a particular type of television programme. The process of beginning privately to question the second-rate nature of all that one has selected to watch is the entry ticket into the realm of cultural opportunities provided by an 'unlimited' media. The empirical finding that the majority of television viewers would prefer *fewer* programmes (see the chapter by Winterhoff-Spurk) gives expression to a helpless protest against what they are in fact doing with the media.

The more objects one collects, the more recommended restaurants one visits, the more journeys one undertakes, and the more one explores one's wishes of every type, in order to satisfy them fully, the more difficult it becomes to close one's eyes to the fact that the basic assumption of the 'rationality of experience' – the manipulation and use of external conditions in order to trigger internal processes of gratification – is questionable. The problem of the discontented pleasure-seekers lies within themselves: in the lack of clarity with which their needs are defined, in the unpredictability of their re-actions, and in their diminishing capability for fascination in the face of the increase in the excitement of what is on offer. Like addicts they grasp after more and more, and gain less and less from what they experience.

The 'powerful' institutions as objects of cultural criticism

Who is responsible for this state of affairs? Cultural critics have been quick to answer this question as if the diagnosis was straight-forward: guilt lies, of course, with the big impersonal forces, above all the powerful economic institutions pursuing their self-interests. What is irritating about this diagnosis is the patronizing relegation of the public to a subordinate role – as if we were too stupid to defend ourselves against temptations and manipulations. In fact, matters are quite different. The 'rationality of experience' consists of the ability to apply our individual intelligence to achieve control over efforts to tempt and manipulate us. Rarely have victims proved so shrewd and capable of defending themselves.

Nevertheless, it remains the case that the media world of the 'experience society' is packed full of temptations, of objects of desire manufactured by big industrial companies. Power to shape culture lies clearly with organizations and institutions, as the history of the mass media demonstrates. Before the first radio stations were established in the United States at the beginning of the 1920s, there was already a network of hundreds of thousands of amateur radio enthusiasts who made their own programmes in a situation of happy chaos. This stage was followed by a wave of commercialization in which large companies swallowed up the amateurs. By the end of 1922 there were five radio stations in the United States; eight months later the number had risen to 450. Since then the electronic media have been ruled by large organizations.

One is tempted to accept this picture of cultural history as the onwards march of cultural industry, of commercialization, and of the colonization of our world of experience – with the solitary satisfaction that remains to the contemporary cultural critic, namely the feeling of being correct.

Loss of power by the institutions; gain of power by the individual

But this feeling is deceptive. In the field of media institutions are losing power over ordinary people. Already in the 1980s and in the early 1990s it was possible to identify signs of a reversal of trend. The basing of television programming decisions on audience ratings figures is nothing other than the systematically conducted attempt by media organizations to suppress their own voice. In effect it suggests that they no longer wish to play a leadership role. What we are witnessing is the spectacle of a process of adaptive competition. It has only avoided leading to a complete subordination of media organizations because audience ratings are a much too problematic and unwieldy instrument of adjustment on which to rely. But it is only with the next phase of technological innovation in media that the tendency to the loss of power by the big media organizations will fully reveal itself for the first time.

We are used to thinking that shifts of power occur in a context of great drama and uproar. Typically, the distribution of power is made into a public issue: those who feel subordinate demand more rights; and the powerful who are threatened prophesy the end of humanity. In the present process of shift of power generated by new media technologies the situation remains confused. The powerful seek to outbid each other in the struggle to gain the controlling position in media. They are in fact participating in a process that is creating the conditions for the diminution of their own power. They are investing huge sums in market research and developing ever more sophisticated methods for discovering what someone might conceivably want. Obedient to the principles of market research they seek to think themselves into the mind of the consumer of tomorrow and come up with products of which people today would not even dream: 'So please, this is what I have invented for you; wouldn't you like to possess it?' In the case of nine out of ten of these new products the consumers decline to be interested and the firms concerned withdraw in as orderly a fashion as possible.

Just as notable is the lack of interest on the part of the gainer of power – individuals. The behaviour of the consumers of media can be only inadequately described by the observation that they have never actively sought out and demanded an increase of their influence, so that they can only with difficulty come to terms with this new and unwanted situation, a situation that they secretly curse. But such an observation helps little: we are each still faced by the situation of taking our lives into our own hands.

The helpless Emperor of China

No: one is not especially happy if one is suddenly made into the Emperor of China. But in the case of the new ruler with the secret desire to continue to be allowed to remain a subject the way back is just as blocked as for the powerful of yesterday. The individual must get used – however unwillingly – to giving answers to terribly difficult questions. First, what do I really want? Second, what opportunities do I have? Third, in what relationship do these incomprehensibly many opportunities stand to what I want? Every one of these questions must confront those who put them with much to contemplate, if not with a crisis of direction and meaning. Provided with the imperial insignia of television viewing guide, of remote control and of the equipment catalogue of the latest superstore for entertainment electronics, the Emperor of China sits on his sofa and becomes acquainted with feelings which are on the whole just as bad as those of his earlier physical deprivation: feelings of helplessness, boredom, sense of meaninglessness, and chronic disappointment.

There is a certain comic touch in contemporary media history. On the one hand, the driving principle of the dynamics of societal change is the goal of a permanent widening of opportunities: but, on the other, ever more people find themselves helpless in the face of this busily created process. Schopenhauer would have found much to make him laugh in this situation. Perhaps from his aphorisms he would have selected the following: 'the time of a man is worth as much as he himself is worth'. In this way he could give expression to his opinion that we were not worth very much.

The end of the diversion from philosophy

The question 'What do I really want?' seems in principle easy to answer. But in reality it always presents us with a puzzle. One knows exactly what one wants when one is hungry, thirsty or cold. But what does one know without the diversion from philosophy provided by unsatisfactory basic living conditions? The widespread idea that every person is provided with an essential core of being that one only has to discover, develop and serve contains a germ of truth. What is naïve, however, is the idea that one has a particular nature from which it is possible to derive exactly what one wants. This error is repeatedly found in our daily self-characterizations ('that's the way I am'), as also in bad psychoanalysis and in traditional market research, which takes an illusory idea of needs as its working basis. What is required in all these areas is a more complex notion that takes into account the openness of people.

Those concerned to explain human behaviour have attributed all sorts of needs to man: a death wish, an innate aggressiveness, an inner need to identify with a territorial group, etc. These sorts of attributes are supposed to belong to the nature of man. In the case of media these attributes are variously defined as sensation-seeking, the desire to be titillated, love of sharing in gossip, mental laziness, being one of the crowd. This discourse on the 'essential' nature of man is sustained by the presumption of a scientific professional basis. It takes the form of the analysis of specific sub-groups – men and women, young and old, black and white – and, at the level of the individual, is reduced to the statement 'Well, that's the way I am'. The tendency to identify the human subject as something concrete and fixed, in this respect as an object, seems to be ineradicable.

But the subject does not exist independently of the way in which it sees itself. We unavoidably *invent* ourselves, however much we may like to act as if we were a given. If one can speak at all of the nature of man, then this nature is most sharply defined by the fact that it is open and uncertain.

Are such considerations too abstract, too divorced from the nature of the problems currently facing media producers, market researchers and audio-visual consumers? Is it not the case that such philosophical considerations have no real importance in the daily life of people? One should treat such questions with caution. In the context in which individuals are having to cope with their daily problems of living amid the reality of 'unlimited' media, it is important to clarify the fundamental point that they cannot expect to find much help from the prescription that they should just be driven by their own nature.

The shock of innovation in information and communication technologies means an end to the condition in which man's daily life has been unburdened of philosophical issues. The comfortable internal logic and momentum of a conceptual model of a social world based on the primacy of technological and economic factors has lost its relevance. No longer can one move about within clearly defined cognitive tracks like the hamster in the revolving wheel. We are entering a situation in which the form of thought in which man has been trained for the last two centuries is no longer of much use to us.

This new situation is usefully described by the title of a film of Jan Troell: *Here's Your Life* (1967). The film seeks to draw attention to the lesson that we must no longer serve institutions and organizations; rather, they are falling over themselves to serve us. We must no longer spend our time with the trivia of perfectionism, because basically all that can be made perfect has already been made perfect. Here you have your life; get on with doing what you want and like to do. What is required is a form of thought that one might perhaps characterize as 'normative intelligence' and which is not to be found in any intelligence test. By 'normative intelligence' is meant the capability to discover what one wants and what is good for oneself and for others.

Is man rational?

'Normative intelligence': one could speak instead of practical reason, being streetwise, using common sense. The term draws our attention back to Immanuel Kant (see Kenneth Dyson's Preface to this book). But various objections can be raised to the employment of the term normative intelligence. From certain sources one might expect to hear that most people are simply too stupid or too deficient in will to meet such demands. Others would be likely to claim that the 'technostructure' has us all so firmly in its grip that it really does not matter what goes on inside our heads. Meanwhile, a third type of critic might announce that it makes no sense to speak of reason; so we had better leave things as they are.

It is tempting to be intimidated by such strongly expressed negative assessments of the potential for practical reason, for the exercise of normative intelligence, in the dawning age of new media. Sympathetically patted on the head by the smiling sceptics of contemporary intellectual culture, we are prone to feel ashamed of our naïvety and to scoff at the idea of practical reason as a juvenile error in the history of philosophy. Practical reason might seem a prime candidate for the museum of historical eccentricities, alongside exorcism!

But practical or moral reasoning cannot be disposed of so quickly or so easily. A weighty counter-argument to the sceptics is the claim that the criticism of reason involves the critic in self-contradiction. We can also argue that, without confidence in our capacity for practical reason, we deny ourselves the ability to act effectively. Because we are alive, and have minds, consciences and wills, we must exploit our capital of practical reasoning. We have no choice.

These arguments are important if we are to evolve a constructive and socially relevant form of thought for the emerging age of new media. It may sound exaggerated, and is in fact only a truism: but our future depends totally on our ability to look at the world rationally, to make judgements of validity and to assume obligations, as Dyson argues in the Preface.

A morphology of irrationality

In what could this practical rationality of conduct reside, and how could one acquire it? The following section of the chapter adopts a dialectical approach: criticism of present media behaviour as the basis for defining appropriate goals to tell us what, as moral beings, we ought to do. It provides a brief morphology of irrationality, in the hope that by this means the requirements of practical reason will be mirrored, albeit in a negative manner. In the search for antitheses to the present situation of media behaviour there is really no alternative to trusting in that which one is seeking, namely in practical or moral reason.

In the attempt to construct a morphology of irrationality two types of argument can be developed: on the one hand, the limited relevance and value of popular models of happiness; and, on the other, widely shared experiences of loss of meaning and alienation.

1. *Popular contemporary models of happiness* have a common denominator: the rationalization of experience. The daily pursuit of happiness associated with these models takes the form of an enormous, unprecedented mobilization of social effort. One has only to observe the preparations for a civic festival: 40 containers delivered, three heavy cranes in action, all in order to install a roller coaster with quadruple loops. Yet this expenditure of energy and materials leads to meagre, often counter-intuitive results. The project of the good life brings to many little more than insecurity, disappointment and, at best, a fleeting happiness. In the final analysis the social and ecological costs of the pursuit of this kind of happiness stand in contrast to a very shallow and meagre psychological benefit.

   At the same time we should beware of jumping to the conclusion that we ought to expel the project of the good life to the periphery of our intellectual concerns and replace it by the principle of renunciation of worldly things. On the contrary: the unlimited scope of opportunities afforded us, which 'post-techno-logical' society has made possible, leaves us with no other choice than to learn somehow or other to make our own happiness.

   Happiness is a collective learning process. We have a lot more to learn. The blueprint that the 'experience society' has drawn up is like one of the first flying machines, which was only able to hop a couple of hundred metres.

2. A second shorthand term of criticism of the way that we live today is *alienation*. In discussions about the contemporary crisis of meaning those who are alienated are presented as helpless and pitiful. But anyone who actively plays a part in his or her own

alienation deserves little sympathy. Two illustrations of this may be useful.

First illustration: *experience provides a substitute for meaning.* Anyone seeking meaning, for instance as a consumer of media, is asking for a product whose quality is supposed to be defined independently of her-/himself: as a relationship between the knowledge that the product offers and reality. However, in the last decades, a new definition of the criterion of quality has taken root – with enormous implications. We no longer measure information, arguments and opinions by the standard of what they convey but by what processes they unleash within us. The desire for pleasure displaces the search for meaning. More important than content becomes the intrinsic interest of the form of dissemination. Pictures, music, voices and charismatic personalities blend perceptually into a form of experience of meaning, in which meaning itself becomes in the final analysis peripheral. Ultimately it is no longer a question of what is being communicated but of whether one is being entertained well or is being bored. Anyone trying to say something of importance about the present and future is drowned in public debate by the voices of those who know how to chatter on endlessly in an amusing and aimless manner.

A second illustration is provided by *virtual meaning.* The idea of cultivating one's worldly wisdom has been displaced by the belief that it is adequate simply to have meaning *available* so that, if the worst comes to the worst, one can fall back on it – consult it. This modern form of stupidity takes the form of the reduction of meaning to the knowledge of where one could go to look for meaning if one should feel the need for it: by consulting appropriate professional opinion, from books, in data archives, by enrolling on educational courses, by making use of institutions like libraries. The new wave of media technology innovation will multiply the 'virtualization' of knowledge. Yet virtual knowledge is not properly or fully understood knowledge; skills that one *could* acquire remain neglected. One believes oneself to be adequately prepared to deal with difficulties by means of one's knowledge of where to go to acquire meaning. But, unfortunately, life is an endless succession of difficulties and requires more resourceful responses than simply relying on seeking out external help.

What follows after the transition to a new era of media?

These antitheses to the contemporary social world provide a useful starting point for looking ahead to the future. It is possible to identify the broad outlines of a future in which ever more technological developments are perfected and in which the power to transform the social world is shifted from the big media institutions to individuals. Many believe that the colonization of life by technology and complex organizations will continue indefinitely. But the assumption that the power of this organizational apparatus can only grow is not very plausible. Like all statements in social theory it is of use only for a specific historical period. But now, on the horizon, a social world is discernible whose character will be determined by the practical reasoning – or lack of it – of the people who inhabit it.

How can one conceive of the cultural history of this future social world? Its character will completely depend on whether we share a capacity to distinguish, if only in a general way, between good sense and stupidity, just as today we share a capability to distinguish between what is technically rational and what is technically irrational.

A system of meaning vouchsafes more security and sense of direction – the more clearly it defines what is an error. The fascination of technological civilization derives above all from the objectivity of its conception of failure. A piece of equipment that does not work, a structure that collapses, a 'maximum credible accident' (MCA), a scientific refutation: these are meaningful results that one can intellectually grasp. Is it possible to restore such certainty of judgement in the 'post-technological' age? The answer seems to be in the negative. What remains to us as the standard depends just on ourselves: with all our hesitations, capriciousness and limitations, on the one hand, but also with our capability for practical or moral reasoning, and for acting with good sense, on the other.

Both of these types of human qualities will find their expression in the cultural dynamics of the future. The long-term historical path of development of a 'post-technological' age oriented to practical reason and common sense cannot, accordingly, be a path of *progress*, comparable with the path followed by technology. More suitable is a model of history that focuses on the continuing threat of a loss of standards. There is an optimum of reason, which is unattainable and which one easily fails to achieve, but in search of which one repeatedly attempts to strive. The most important cognitive principle in this respect is the capacity for critical reasoning: the ability to recognize what constitutes unacceptably bad behaviour, to apprehend what is feeble-minded, something that every alert child can manage.

There are always causes for doubt about the way in which we live, and new doubts are always arising. By now it should be clear why the question of the future in the 'post-technological' society is systematically connected with a critique of the present. Doubt about the way in which we live throws into bold relief the agenda of practical reasoning. A concrete prognosis is hidden away in this thesis. The two above-mentioned main contemporary themes of cultural criticism – of counter-productive models of happiness, and of illusions of meaning – have the potential to serve as means of creating a new social dynamism. They have this potential because, in both respects, we have so distanced ourselves from practical reason that it is hurting us.

However, such a prognosis of cultural dynamism by no means represents a mechanistic law. Hence the question arises of what we can do today to *encourage* this cultural dynamism, and what we are doing to *hinder it*. With this question in mind, the final part of this chapter is concerned with the rapid commercialization of the media world, in whose wake the public-service broadcasting institutions have already been caught up for some time.

Kirch meets Adorno

In 1994 one could read in the German newspapers that Germany's most powerful commercial media player, Leo Kirch, had accused the Federal President's Commission on the State of Television of lacking expert knowledge. Even if this accusation is not sustainable, there is an underlying message to this criticism: that you cannot overlook the most vital factor at work in contemporary television, namely the economic and industrial forces at work. Proposals for the future of television lack a solid basis if they derive from one simply fixing one's attention on one value or another, in the process ignoring the economic dimension of broadcasting. Interestingly, a remarkably similar form of argument can be found in the work of neo-Marxist critical theory, expressed of course with different words and against the background of an opposed normative position. A surprising alliance appears: between Kirch and Theodor Adorno. Their common position takes the form of arguing that television is a cultural industry and functions in the way we have experienced it in the last ten years. There are only two possibilities available: join in or get out of the industrial game of broadcasting; use the commercial opportunities or turn one's back in disgust. Is this form of argument persuasive?

A reassessment of the critique of commercialization

In recent decades there has been no shortage of critiques of the commercialization of the media, but what has been lacking is a critique of these critiques. Little is gained, other than avoiding the need to think by embracing the formula that commercialization of broadcasting is basically an evil. This formula has become almost an intellectual reflex action. Such an intellectual position may be comfortable. But it adds nothing in the form of providing a sense of meaning and direction in contemporary society, for the option of abolishing commercialization of the media is simply not available. Commercialization does not mean the inevitable implementation of technical or economic imperatives without consideration of cultural costs. In the investment goods industry, or for instance in the steel sector, situations may arise in which there is precisely *one* correct decision that is readily identifiable by specialist engineers; any other decision would put one's professional reputation at risk. But in the consumer goods industry, and more recently in the media industry, strategic considerations must take a much freer form. To put it another way, the entrepreneur is forced to consider ways of liberating her-/himself from the limitations of practical imperatives – because the entrepreneur in this sector is dealing not with things but with people.

What people want from the media, by which media contents they are moved – these are not as readily predictable as the fodder requirements of a factory farm for fattening chickens. In contrast to the factory farm worker the media entrepreneur conducts her/his business in conditions, some of which are clear-cut and others of which are open and ambiguous. On the one hand, the criteria of economic success are fully clear. On the other, it is often unclear by which cultural means these criteria of economic success can best be achieved. A focus on the special difficulties that confront the entrepreneur in the media sector suggests that in many respects the present media landscape could be improved – and that in the process it could be improved in a cultural sense. For this reason a critique of the commercialization of media ought to operate from the outset with the weapons of economics itself.

An economic critique of the audience rating system

The invitation to exercise practical reason can be supported by economic argument. But the media world still refuses to accept this invitation. The present system of 'ratings-oriented' television rests, first and foremost, on its claim to be economically rational. But the millions spent on advertising are not cost-effective, not least because the programmes that they finance are not worth viewing. Although the audience rating system is kept alive by economic actors, it must be asked whether 'ratings-oriented' television can be economic in the long term. Someone in love makes himself more and more a figure of fun to the object of his attentions – the further he goes in his efforts at wooing. Similarly, television appears more and more tiresome, obtrusive and insistent the further it goes in trying to subordinate itself to the moods of the public. Television is already no longer as loved as it was in the 1960s and 1970s. The worst scenario facing media companies is apathy. Television viewers zap from channel to channel and leave the set on in the corner of the room without watching it. Whole groups of consumers threaten to break away, above all the better educated and the financially most powerful.

The seductive aspect of the audience rating system is its clarity. It represents an intelligently conceived and executed project by means of which media institutions condemn themselves to stupidity. They can congratulate themselves on having a rigorous mechanism of thought and being able to quantify precisely the difference between 'good' and 'bad' programmes. But, in doing so, they are succumbing to the magical – and deceptive – charms of clarity. From then on they come simply to *believe* in the economic rationale of the audience rating system. The media institutions' desire to rid themselves of the fear of uncertainty by relying on the audience rating system triumphs over the fear of ineffective and inefficient media performance.

Television's discourse with the public, conducted via the audience rating system, is reminiscent of a married couple, only one of whom is allowed to speak and act, while the other has only the possibility of registering approval or disagreement on a scale of 0–100 per cent. The belief that the second partner would ever get exactly what he/she wanted is patent nonsense.

Arguments against the thesis of an imperative

But the impact of innovation in information and communication technologies will create a new context in which it will be possible to reconcile arguments about what is economically rational with arguments about what is morally reasonable. It is possible to conceive of a media world in which information services and education programmes will earn more money than 'infotainment', in which more demanding cultural products will be as easy to sell as simple ones, in which there will be a demand not only for immediate gratification but also for more challenging and reflective programmes. Good examples are provided by Channel Four in Britain and TVW Seven in Australia. In 1994 these television channels were awarded the Carl Bertelsmann Prize for 'social responsibility in television'. Notably, the common feature of the two channels is that both are financed exclusively by advertising revenue. The impending impact of technological innovation could strengthen the economic attraction of treating media viewers and users as people possessing practical reason. This new attraction would be the product of two factors: first, because the media institutions' perceptions of consumers are altered and improved by the arrival of interactive media; and, secondly, because the consumers are in effect compelled to adopt a more active and more critical attitude not only by the sheer scale of choice available but also by the extension of direct forms of financing programmes, like pay-per-view.

Beyond media policy

Ultimately, whether there will be an economic pressure to reconcile commercial calculations with a new respect for the practical reason of the viewer and user depends on us. It will be determined, in the final analysis, by whether we choose to be guided by practical or moral reasoning. If it is the case that power is shifting to us as viewers and users of media, then we must reflect in new and different ways about media policy. The current discussion about media policy is dominated by the media institutions and organizations. In the process one media policy issue is shockingly neglected, even though its importance is increasing with the impact of technological innovation – namely the education of media users.

This reference to the critical importance of the education of media users is not intended to refer to what is generally understood as media studies. The notion of specialized media studies is, if anything, a hindrance in this respect. Practices of moral reasoning and common sense in the use of media cannot be instilled by means of such a specialized course of study. These practices are a matter of education in its totality. The requirement of education of media users draws attention to tasks which appear soluble and yet utopian. Soluble, because they do not demand major new financial investments, only a change of educational practice; and utopian for the reason that few things are more difficult than to change the practice of education. But it is precisely here, in the relations between parents and children, in the nursery schools, in primary and secondary education and in further and higher education, that everything will be decided. Whoever reflects politically about the media culture of the future must venture into areas far beyond classical media policy (as Hoffmann-Riem stresses) and current media studies.

The woman on the sofa

In one of Isaac B. Singer's novels the following scene occurs. While the main character is waiting in a strange apartment for the arrival of the landlord, he catches sight of the lady of the house through a half-opened door. She is reclining on the sofa and is skimming through fashion magazines. The hidden observer knows that she has been doing this for ever and a day and asks himself whether she will continue to do this for the rest of her life. He answers in the affirmative – because what else can she do? But what will she occupy herself with in the next world? She cannot skim through fashion magazines for the rest of eternity! The observer sinks into philosophizing.

This scene can be read as a symbol of our present situation. We are the woman on the sofa, but we are also the observer. It is the philosophizing observer in us who will decide whether it will occur to us to do anything other than skim through fashion magazines.

4

The Ethics of Media Use: Media Consumption as a Moral Challenge

HERMANN LÜBBE

The central argument of this chapter is that the ethics of the use of media have become far more important than the ethics of the media themselves and the regulatory framework that governs their activities. This argument does not amount to saying that the ethics of the media are now irrelevant. We should still continue to hope for signs of improvements in the moral intelligence that the media display as they attempt to fulfil their purposes of entertainment, education and information. It remains of ethical relevance that media decision makers are, to some extent at least, motivated by public-interest considerations (see the chapter by Hoffmann-Riem). However, in a context in which such motivations cannot be guaranteed, the primary ethical question becomes a matter of the consumers of media making the best use that they can of the ever more pervasive presence of the media in their daily lives and of the advantages and disadvantages of living in our 'media-saturated' age. 'Best use' means basing media consumption behaviour on relevant, effective, self-defined rules for dealing with the obtrusive presence of the media. Basically, the prospects for reconciling media and ethics depend on the adequacy of these self-defined rules for guiding how we use our daily time and conduct our lives: in other words, on the question of whether – and to what extent – individuals seek to live a moral life.

It would be a gross error to assume that the legal regulations, which provide a framework of order for media operators, can relieve us – as consumers of media – from the requirements of moral self-determination. Of course, these legal regulations for the media – along with requirements that follow from general laws, as Hoffmann-Riem emphasizes – provide an indispensable, albeit very broad framework. From the protection of young people to the protection of those with religious beliefs from remarks offensive to their feelings there has, for good reason, been an attempt to ensure that the appropriate rules are optimal with respect to their compatibility with the principle of the freedom of the press. In fact, there would be some very odd – and ultimately unsustainable – situations in families and in other social groups, in relationships among neighbours and in schools, if we allowed ourselves to tolerate behaviour in these intimate areas of social life that has routinely come to be offered in the media.

One can express the same point in the following way: the social controls which are concerned to cultivate good morals in our daily relations with each other operate far more rigorously than the social controls which – consistent with the principle of freedom of the press – are supposed to represent the way in which we in the media ought to behave in relation to other people or groups of people.

But, above all else, the following point holds with respect to the relationship between media and ethics: that the supposed and empirically substantiated effects of media contents are dwarfed by the effects, individually and collectively, that derive from habits of usage of the media. As Winterhoff-Spurk shows, these habits are formed by, and can be remade by, media consumers. The effects of the media vary much more strongly according to the habitual ways in which individuals or groups relate to the media than by virtue of their information or entertainment content. For this reason an effective morality of media usage is culturally more important than a good media morality.

One must not, of course, forget that the knowledge of how one ought to act and live, in other words the possession of an ethics, does not automatically mean that individuals are capable of acting and living in a moral manner. Moralists have always known that the preaching of morals is not sufficient to give effect to morality. The same point applies to the morality of media usage. It would be naïve to suppose that it could be possible to inculcate moral competence in media use simply by drawing attention to the advantages to one's life from taking care to respect moral rules, however eloquently the message was expressed. How we actually deal with the media is dependent, more than anything else, on the influences from family and other intimate social milieu, influences to which we are exposed especially in our childhood and teenage years. Here is a standard theme of media studies and one which media education seeks to articulate and counteract.

But the need for an ethics of media usage is not affected by this fact of influence from intimate social milieu. The validity of moral rules does not vary according to the greater or lesser extent of compliance with them: for the strength of the foundations of a morality remains indifferent to any social or temporal variations in compliance.

Virtue in media use: entertainment and happiness

By far the most important moral rule, whose indispensability forces itself on every consumer of media, is that of continuing to consume media in moderation. What we mean by virtue is practised skill in complying with moral rules, and moderation belongs clearly to the traditional cardinal virtues. No new justification in principle is needed for the argument that any lifestyle that fails to take account of such virtues will come to grief. That kind of knowledge is common-sense knowledge. The experiences of life on which this knowledge is based are old and, irrespective of their age, have not dated. In other words, these virtues are classical.

Nevertheless, there is a change in the conditions of life which reinforces to us the sense of the indispensability of virtue. As far as the virtue of moderation is concerned, this reinforcement is provided by the fact that we are living in a time of growing plenty in the media, indeed of mounting over-abundance. In times when social welfare seems to be more securely guaranteed, and prospects for a longer life improved, health becomes a problem whose solution seems to depend primarily on developing adequate practical skills in self-defining one's lifestyle, in other words in behaving in a moral manner. The preoccupation with acquiring these skills is apparent in the advice columns of women's and family magazines.

The same point applies in dealing with the problem of over-supply with which we are confronted today as media consumers. This over-supply of media does not become a moral problem because of the supposed or even actual immoral contents of the media but as a consequence of their preoccupation with entertainment and the way in which that seduces the consumer into passivity.

The art of entertainment and the entertaining arts remain an indispensable part of every culture. It should not be forgotten that the appeal to moderation in using the media for entertainment is not a matter of harsh and embittered moral preaching. In fact, moral preaching has become a characteristic of parts of media entertainment. Who has not had the experience of seeking to relax in front of a popular detective story on television, only to find that, with deliberate moral intent, one has been uncovered as subconsciously racist? The initial presumption, to which one found oneself drawn, that the gypsy had committed the crime was finally undermined by the evidence that the crime had in fact been perpetrated by the 'respectable' accountant.

An ethics of media usage has, in other words, nothing against entertainment: a point parallel to that made by Dyson in Chapter 8. The problem resides almost exclusively in the moral difficulty of practising moderation in our daily lives. If we can succeed in dealing with that difficulty, then – by contrast – the immorality of the contents of many entertainment programmes, for instance in the youth subculture, is rendered almost completely unimportant. To put the argument another way: the destructive effects of the immoderate consumption of entertainment programmes also occur when the contents of these programmes, for instance in the form of old-fashioned detective stories, are gushing with sound morality. The same conclusion applies: the morality of media consumers is much more important for the future of our culture than the morality of the media.

Why does immoderate consumption of the media produce destructive effects? Quite simply, it makes individuals incapable of acting like, and being, free persons. Never before have people lived so freely as in modern welfare societies. This statement is not rhetorical hyperbole, but rather an empirically sustainable, quantifiable proposition. As Theodor Adorno said, time and money are standards by which we can measure freedom. There were never such clear indicators of the widening opportunities available to us, and such rich opportunities into the bargain, as are available to us today.

The challenge of freedom is essentially moral in nature. This challenge takes the form of using freedom to make sense of, and ultimately to give meaning to, our lives by means of self-determined action. The degree of capability to activate ourselves in this way that is required of us was never greater than today. Most seriously of all, the excess in media consumption of entertainment destroys exactly this capability by inducing passivity.

'The media' is now a collective name for very heterogeneous things. From the point of view of an ethics of media consumption they can be differentiated according to the degree of activity which is required from us, even in relation to the consumption of entertainment. In this respect television is the most effortless medium, and precisely for that reason the most used. The effort to pay attention that is required of someone listening to the radio is considerably greater. For readers – as Homolka's chapter demonstrates – the effort is even more demanding, even on the modest level of media performance associated with the reading matter in weekly magazines. On the other hand, those who have learnt to find delight in the active enjoyment of specialist subject books, biographies, historical works, comprehensive reference books, and even 'elitist' art books, have accomplished a feat of self-determination on the highest level, seen from the perspectives of motivation, time management and co-ordination of action.

This accomplishment explains at the same time why readers of books are the 'happiest' of media consumers. As part of the teaching of virtue, the teaching of happiness is also classical – which means old but, nevertheless, not outdated. It states that happiness is not to be gained by directly pursuing happiness as a goal. Happiness appears as a side-effect of proper, meaningful conduct, especially when this conduct makes demands on our powers – psychological and moral. It is, in other words, dependent on our capacity for moral self-determination.

Virtue in media use: news and current affairs and good citizenship

Significant practical consequences for our lives follow from our capacities as individuals (even if that capacity is not fully realized) to marshal resistance to the temptations to engage in excessive consumption of media entertainment. The young victims of long periods spent immersed in the world of Walkmans, of computer games and of videos seem a striking manifestation of a newly emerging phenomenon. But, in fact, this phenomenon has affected our intellectual culture for a long time. We have exposed ourselves to masses of information: to newspaper coverage of world events, their illustration in the form of the vivid immediacy of television pictures, supplementary current affairs programmes and newspaper commentary, the recall of this mass of information in the form of the reading matter contained in weekly illustrated magazines and television programmes. In doing so we have thought that we were fulfilling the requirement for the politically engaged, critical citizen to be properly informed.

However, even the consumption of news, as it figures in most people's daily use, mainly serves the purpose of entertainment. The passivity which educationalists and sociologists diagnose as the effect of excessive consumption of entertainment on the personality is illustrated in the excessive consumption of news – a consumption that bears no real relationship to the intellectual content of news reporting. This phenomenon can be readily observed. There are students who conscientiously seek to read news magazines like *The Economist* or *Time* from cover to cover each week as well as their daily and Sunday newspapers. For the same reason, it seems essential to tune into talk shows in order to expose oneself to the best informed opinions from the top national and international intellectuals. Similarly, by tuning into the popular screen adaptations of the 'great works' that one read, or was expected to read, in school literature lessons, we seem to be offered an opportunity for all sorts of reflection on the aesthetics of drama.

The sad truth is that, above and beyond the substantial amount of entertainment value to be derived from such heavy media consumption, this chaotic reception of information is almost completely irrelevant. Our capacity for political judgement in no way grows in proportion to the extent of our consumption of news. There is also no real increase in other skills. In order to be informed about world events for the rest of the day it is generally sufficient to read the headlines at breakfast time or to tune into the early morning radio news. Evening television news only illustrates what one already knows, generally in an entertaining manner. There is no objection to doing that for a quarter of an hour or so; beyond that it is just a matter of killing time.

This outcome arises from the fact that the reception of news and information is normally of importance in extending one's competence only when it takes place in the context of concrete, practical and well-defined activities – for instance, being engaged in education in its various forms or in corporate or community decision-making.

In making this point I do not claim that media dedicated to the provision of news are irrelevant for cultural or political purposes. I mean only that one should wake up to the fact that the consumption of news, both in its scale and content, needs to be governed by some practical criteria related to one's field of activity. In absorbing this lesson one is also learning that, without a competent use of the mass media, one is not really capable of playing an active role in important social and political, let alone job-related, discourse and decision-making.

Use of mass media as a factor of cultural differentiation

It is vital to appreciate just how powerful are the cultural, social and political consequences of the attempt to give practical meaning in our daily lives to a morality of media consumption, with its emphasis on moderation (or indeed of the consequences of failing to do so). These consequences are not confined to the virtual reality defined by the pious wishes of moralists. They are discernible in the here and now, forcing themselves in an empirical manner on our attention. One of the standard arguments of cultural pessimists – shared by the Frankfurt School of critical theory – takes the form of the thesis that the mass media have the effect of destroying individuality and identity. They are, in other words, homogenizing in a cultural sense and, in the process, depress cultural standards. In reality the opposite is the case. The mass media are in fact unleashing complex processes of cultural differentiation. They are driving apart levels of cultural participation, are making differences of skill and competence more conspicuous, and are favouring the formation of élites. What is at work here is primarily the cumulative effects of different levels and types of media use by consumers. This process of cultural differentiation is based on different forms and styles of time management, reflecting the morality of media use. There are plenty of examples of the various ways in which levels of cultural participation are being driven apart: according to quality of information and capacity for judgement, according to knowledge and expertise, and according to common sense and skills in dealing with everyday life. The crucial distinction is between activity and passivity, as revealed by playing sport in the evening instead of just watching football on the television; going out to garden instead of watching endless boring television series; rehearsing in a brass band practice instead of just listening to another music programme on the radio; carefully reading the specialist reports in the economics pages of the daily newspaper about the content and effects of health policy reforms instead of just listening to the exchange of views in the appropriate television talk show; attending a weekly further education course rather than reading moralizing magazine articles; participating in local citizen action groups instead of having a disillusionment with politics increased by too much media consumption of politics as 'talking heads'; making an effort to acquire facts instead of relying on answers to interviewers' questions; getting hold of relevant statistics instead of listening to politicians demonstrating their convictions on television; or getting involved in local and regional historical studies instead of just listening to a recital of problems in far-off countries.

What we are talking about is not something imminent but something that has been a manifest reality for some time. The opportunities for media use are distributed in an egalitarian manner. But the means of media use are extremely differentiated, depending on unevenly distributed competences and skills of media use. Hence it is important to underline the point that the so-called 'mass society' is developing today in quite the opposite direction from that originally conceived by cultural critics.

Conclusion

This chapter has argued that the morality of media usage now belongs to the most important cultural competences on which the individual is reliant for providing practical guidance in her/his daily life. This conclusion leads on to a related question: which factors are decisive in determining whether, in the conduct of our daily lives, we are successful in putting into practice the well-known (because simple) rules of media use, with their emphasis on moderation in the consumption of media entertainment? The answer is painful. By far the most important of these factors are those relating to the social milieu in which one grows up, especially one's peer groups and, most of all, the family milieu. The prospects of cultural homogenization of these milieus are in fact becoming smaller in societies integrated by mass media. What this means is that the inequality of our individual level of media culture and competence increases in a self-reinforcing process. The problems that derive from this process are of such a scale as to undermine any confidence in the adequacy of our present, however commendable, media education as a remedy.

Note

This chapter was originally published as 'Mediennutzungsethik: Medienkonsum als moralische Herausforderung' in H. Hoffmann (ed.), *Gestern begann die Zukunft*, Darmstadt: Wissenschaftliche Buchgesellschaft, 1994, pp. 313–18.

5

Coping with Plenty: Psychological Aspects of Television and Information Overload

PETER WINTERHOFF-SPURK

Stress, strain, infarct: the individual in the information age

Current social developments are often looked at from the point of view of information and communication theory: and, correspondingly, there is at present much talk about the 'information explosion' or about 'an information age'.[1] Such diagnoses are substantiated by statistics. Thus, 30.8 million daily newspapers, 2.1 million weekly newspapers, 122.1 million magazines and 16.5 million professional journals were sold in Germany in the third quarter of 1993. Moreover, 67,277 new or reprinted book titles, 288 new films and about 213 million records/CDs were sold in 1992.[2] Finally, 227 radio and about 50 television programmes could be received in Germany in 1993.[3] Each year's production was being added to the books, newspapers, video films and records/CDs already existing. The average German engages in the use of audio-visual media about six hours a day; according to the German Foundation for Reading (Stiftung Lesen), one hour and forty minutes, in which people read various print media, can be added to this total.[4] Thus, a German spends almost eight hours a day absorbing media – nearly as much time as is spent sleeping or working.

Such an increase of potentially relevant information – fuelled by the development and introduction of new media technologies – leads to speculation about the consequences for the individual of having to deal with all this information. It can be assumed that information 'garbage' leads to information stress and information strain, in the worst case even to information infarct.[5] We have to ask what the science of human experience and behaviour, psychology, has to say about these alarming prospects and what the implications of this answer are for the issue of moral standards in the emerging age of multimedia.[6]

We will try to answer this question in this chapter. First, we describe some general results and theories of cognitive psychology concerning perception and processing of information by the individual. Then we will develop these findings and ideas by dealing with the following media psychological problem: how do people process information while watching television? Our reflections on this topic will be put into more concrete terms by our explanation of the reception of news. Finally, we want to discuss the question of whether, and to what extent, the 'competent' viewer can contribute to avoiding the above-mentioned media threats of stress, strain and infarct. What light does our knowledge of how people actually use television throw on the question of moral standards?

From perception to cognition: the human being as an information processing system

Cognitive psychology is concerned to describe and explain human behaviour as a processing of information. In this context the human being is 'understood as a system, which assimilates, stores, processes and produces information and which thereby uses its knowledge and pursues objectives'.[7] Here the term 'information' has a special meaning: all external stimuli ('environmental stimulation') which have an influence on the individual and for which there is a corresponding sensorium are considered to be information.[8] (For our purpose we can ignore the fact that internal stimuli like hunger, pain, movement of muscles, etc. can be taken as information according to this definition.) If we understand information in the way defined above, information will be depicted, united and worked on in one way or the other in the human brain. These 'internal images' of information are termed 'cognitions' in psychology; they are, so to speak, the 'elements of thinking'.

The route from information to cognition is at present theoretically reconstructed in the following steps: (a) perception, (b) sensory storing, (c) storing in short-term memory, and (d) storing in long-term memory.[9] This process will now be explained in terms of visual information processing. This type of information processing can be divided into (a) visual perception, (b) iconic memory, (c) short-term memory and (d) long-term memory.

(a) Human beings learn about 90 per cent of the information from their environment with their eyes.[10] However, only on a small part of the retina – on the *fovea centralis* – are external objects depicted sharply. Since only a few objects can be grasped at a glance, human beings have to move the eye in such a way that the object to be observed is – if possible – always depicted exactly in this spot.[11] Between three and five fixations can take place in a second (during the movement of the eye information cannot be assimilated). Altogether, a human being is able to process at the most 300,000 different visual stimuli per day (16 waking hours = 57,600 seconds multiplied by 5 fixations per second = 288,000 stimulus-configurations). In other words, visual perception is always selective.

The selection follows two principles. (A) 'Bottom-up' or 'data-driven perception' uses specific characteristics of the object perceived – that means of the picture. These specific characteristics are newness or complexity, the amount of the stimulus or its intensity, its movement, colour, the contrast with the environment or a position at a prominent place of the range of vision (e.g. on the top left). Stimuli with a signalling function (the faces of babies, a person's name, erotic stimuli, the word 'danger!', etc.) attract visual attention. (B) 'Top-down' or 'concept-driven perception' results from the conditions in which the person perceiving is operating. Such conditions may be, for example, acute deficits of the organism (like pain, hunger, thirst, heat, etc.), more complex necessities (curiosity, sexuality, etc.), or interests, expectations, attitudes or motives.

(b) The information perceived in this way is stored almost completely for a period of about 250–500 milliseconds (visual sensory register, iconic memory or sensoric buffer). As long as it is available there, it can be processed on a higher level. But if attention is not directed to it, information gets lost almost unused.

(c) Visual information, to which the individual directs her/his attention, is available (together with other information) for about 15 seconds in the working memory. This is valid only in cases of a limited amount of information (about seven chunks) so that the capacity can be improved by repetitions, forming of clusters or production of associations (mnemonic aids). If this period expires with the information unused, it will be either forgotten or replaced by new information.

(d) Information which is repeated often and which is relevant or to which attention is directed is stored in long-term memory and connected with other cognitions, which need not be visual ones (i.e. multimodal coding).[12] Different levels of processing can be distinguished.[13] The more intensively a cognition is worked on, that is, integrated into available knowledge, the better it will be remembered. The visual long-term memory in particular is capable of extraordinary performances. In an investigation persons were shown 600 pictures in one hour. After a short period of time the test persons recognized about 97 per cent, and after a week 87 per cent of the pictures.[14] In a different investigation the participants identified 73 per cent of 10,000 pictures shown before.[15]

To return to the question of information strain, the psychological analysis of visual assimilation and processing of information shows that a human being has only limited sensory and cognitive capacities. Thus he/she cannot perceive all visual stimuli in the environment, because the eye can carry out five fixations per second at most. The (subjective) environment, already perceived in a reduced manner compared with the (objective) environment of stimuli, is only stored for about half a second in the sensory visual memory. Only seven units of information reach the working memory, and only a few of them are transferred to the long-term memory after specific cognitive processes. It seems that less and less information is cognitively processed on the way from a relatively complete perception to an elaborated storing.

But how does a human being react once he/she is faced with amounts of information he/she cannot process completely any more? Is there evidence for the above-mentioned development from strain to infarct?

This question is dealt with in cognitive psychology under the key term 'focusing of attention'. Human beings are able to use their limited cognitive resources flexibly according to current demands (the model of flexible allocation of resources).[16] Where a task is difficult, the largest amount of capabilities for processing is used for it; only a little capacity remains to carry out other tasks simultaneously. In order to describe this process with regard to the processing of visual information the metaphor of the spotlight was used.[17] Without special demands, the spotlight of attention is set relatively wide and grasps a large area of the environment. Stimuli out of the spotlight's scope are not lighted up at all; those within its scope are only weakly lighted up. Only by means of the already-mentioned 'bottom-up' or 'top-down' demands does the light focus on a small area, which is then illuminated.

At the same time the flexible allocation of resources permits the human being to deal with larger amounts of information. The human being can (A) decide, after a first, superficial processing, not to make available any cognitive resources (active avoidance) or to concentrate only on certain information (selective allocation of attention). It can (B) integrate detailed information into larger units (chunking). Or it can (C) integrate configurations of information, which occur often, into cognitive structures of a higher order such as so-called schemes, scripts, prototypes, frames and stereotypes.[18] Their renewed identification and treatment will be automated according to the experiences of the learner and will thereby require fewer cognitive resources.

Information stress will only occur if all these mechanisms are not effective any more (for example if many new, intensive items of information have to be processed which are contradictory in themselves or which contradict schemes which already exist and/or change rapidly and are relevant at the same time), and if simultaneously the corresponding environment of stimuli cannot be abandoned. Like any other kind of stress, information stress causes particular patterns of behaviour (coping strategies) and in extreme cases even the breakdown of the capacity for processing information.[19]

From selection of programme to mood management: television as processing of information

We are now going to transfer the general ideas of cognitive psychology about the processing of information to the specific situation of a television viewer. How do human beings deal with the amount of programmes on offer?[20]

In order to describe this problem we asssume the following order of events for adults. After a first decision to switch on the television, the viewer has to come to a decision about the channel selection – unless he/she has already done this. Channel selection can be decided on the basis of a complete or incomplete search in a television programme guide, or it can be decided by using, for example, the remote control. If the search is successfully brought to a close, the viewer will switch to the chosen channel and for the time being stick to it. The basic assumption is that viewers will come to the decision about channel selection by being active, adequately informed and oriented to an objective, as well as on the basis of their permanent characteristics of personality ('traits') and/or present states and needs ('states').

These bases of decision at the viewer's disposal are investigated in the 'uses-and-gratification approach'.[21] Roberts and Bachen list the following characteristics, which can be found in the literature on the topic: 'Surveillance, excitement, reinforcement, guidance, anticipated communication, relaxation, alienation, information acquisition, interpretation, tension reduction, social integration, social and parasocial interaction, entertainment, affective guidance, behavioural guidance, social contact, self and personal identity, reassurance, escape, and so on . . . '.[22] Independent of the motives or combination of motives of the individual viewer or of a group of viewers in coming to a decision is the following: in seeking the satisfaction of his needs the viewer actively uses television for general or specific programmes.[23]

The next question concerns the planned or unplanned use of television. A planned switching on of television can concern either specific programmes always shown on television at the same time (programme loyalty) or specific channels (channel loyalty). English and American studies show clear evidence of programme loyalty for soap-operas and news.[24] Channel loyalty means that the viewer prefers one channel compared to other channels; though channel loyalty is not as strong as programme loyalty. A second aspect of channel loyalty is that the viewer sticks to the chosen channel even for the next programme ('lead-in' or 'audience inheritance' effect). This effect can govern more than half of the viewers of the preceding programme.[25]

In the case of the unplanned use of television the viewer has to come to a decision about the choice of programme spontaneously.[26] For information he can use print media, electronic media and other television viewers. In several American studies at the end of the 1980s it was shown that the people surveyed made almost daily use of print media in choosing programmes; in fact, they made more intensive use of the print media the more programmes were available.[27] In one study, between 80 and 90 per cent of the people interviewed looked for the time when the programme began, for the channel, for information about the contents, for programmes that other channels offered at the same time and for the title of the programme in television guides.[28] Surprisingly, knowledge about stars and guests (in shows) was relevant for only about 40 per cent of viewers. About 50 per cent came to the decision about the choice of programme only after having switched on the television.[29]

In the Federal Republic of Germany, between around 60 per cent (according to one survey) and 75–83 per cent (according to others) of people asked inform themselves by reading television guides or supplements to daily newspapers.[30] Between 18 per cent (in one survey) and 45.6 per cent (in another) get hints from daily newspapers.[31] According to a study by the Bayerischer Rundfunk, nearly half of the people asked decide spontaneously which programme they want to watch.[32]

If viewers seek out a programme when already watching television, the following aspects can be distinguished:[33]

1. *Procedure*:
    automatic: search in numerical order of channels
    controlled: search in planned, but not numerical order
    (e.g. according to preference of channels)
2. *Search repertoire*:
    elaborated: complete or nearly complete search
    restricted: incomplete search
3. *Evaluation*:
    complete: search on all channels, return to the best option
    limited: search on channels up to the first acceptable option

Two patterns of unplanned search are described in the study by Heeter which has already been referred to several times: automatic (numerical order) and elaborated (complete) search, on the one hand; and controlled (not numerical) and restricted (incomplete) search, on the other.[34] Those people who preferred the automatic/ elaborated strategy also preferred the complete evaluation, whereas those who used the controlled/restricted strategy preferred the limited evaluation. But, based on results obtained from psychological research on decision-making, it can be assumed that even the complete search will be replaced by simpler individual heuristics and strategies in time – for example by having a look at some preferred channels in numerical order.[35] Neumann assesses this number at about seven plus/minus two.[36]

It is clear, then, that the individual is not flooded by an overwhelming provision of television programmes. He/she selects appropriate programmes with the help of variable strategies, on the basis of her/his needs and expectations and influenced by the specific situation and previous experiences in watching television.

Watching television starts by the viewer looking at the set (visual attention or contact rate). This behaviour is extremly variable according to programme, culture and group of recipients. American investigations indicate for adults an average contact rate of 65.3 per cent of the total time of transmission: features achieved the highest (77.9 per cent) and commercial programmes the lowest rate (51.8 per cent).[37] Studies from England indicate 63 per cent for men and 54 per cent for women; commercial programmes again attained the lowest values.[38] For the Federal Republic of Germany, during the period from 6.00 p.m. to 10.30 p.m. the contact rate varied between 20 and 75 per cent (weather report).[39] Between 8.00 p.m. and 9.00 p.m. the rate always amounts to more than 70 per cent. Infants younger than one year pay no attention at all to television; the contact rate achieves its highest value (more than 70 per cent) for nine-year-olds, and goes down to about 60 per cent for adults.

The time spent in front of the television set and the time spent watching television are not identical. According to an American investigation, based on information provided by the parents, a child spent 40 hours per week in front of the television set; in fact, it watched for only 3.4 hours during this time – as the analysis of video recordings of the child confirmed.[40] Though this may appear an extreme case, the average for all analysed cases amounts to 3.2 hours per week. Children look away, for example, if the dialogue of adults (especially of men), conventional forms of visual presentation such as cuts, zooms and pans, and long, complicated speeches are shown.[41] Furthermore, other activities distract attention. According to an investigation by Levy, 41 per cent of the people surveyed eat while watching television; between 20 per cent and 25 per cent read books and newspapers, talk to other members of the family or do their homework.[42] Other studies discovered that 72 per cent of the viewers are occupied with other, so-called secondary activities during the news.[43] Again eating and drinking rank first, achieving a value of 45 per cent, followed by reading and writing (30 per cent), housework (26 per cent) and conversation (4 per cent). In another study 37 per cent of the participants talk to each other while watching television and 35 per cent eat and smoke at the same time. [44] In the study by Kubey and Csikszentmihalyi 37.5 per cent of the single viewers said that they eat while they watch television.[45] For Germany several representative opinion polls of the BAT Freizeitforschungsinstitut show that about 60 per cent of the viewers are occupied by other activities while watching television. Thus, watching television becomes a secondary activity instead of remaining a primary activity.

Finally, the ends of programmes or breaks caused by inserted television advertisements lead attentive and interested viewers to look away from the set, to put on another channel or to take up a different occupation. American investigations show that viewers who have access to cable television put on a different channel especially at the beginning and at the end of a programme or if advertisements are shown.[46] About half of the young viewers and about a quarter of the adults switched to a different channel as soon as television advertisements were shown.[47]

However, the contact rate represents only a first approach towards understanding the cognitive process mentioned above, because neither eye movements nor processes of storing can be recorded in this way. Investigations of the eye movements of viewers are primarily carried out in the psychology of public relations.[48] It turns out that eye movements relate to the characteristics mentioned above, such as newness or complexity, amount and intensity of the stimuli, movement, colour, contrast to the environment, a position at a preferred place of the range of vision (e.g. on the top left), and stimuli with the function of a signal. With the help of these studies it has been possible to investigate, for example, whether children watching educational programmes look in the right place at the right moment.[49] Kroeber-Riehl sums up this research as follows: 'Eyes are caught by those elements of a picture which create by their motive an "event of the content" or by their shape a "visual event".'[50]

Eye movement is not only 'data-driven'; it is also a result of attitudes, expectations and mental states of the viewers. The 'visual schemes' of viewers (for example of a 'typical' state visit, of a 'typical' welcome at an airport) are certainly of importance as well. They guide attention and make recognition easier. The perception of a picture guided by a visual scheme can even go so far that persons in an experiment to test the ability of memorizing identify pictures in the strongly standardized terms of pictures seen before, although they did not occur in the film that was the subject of the test.[51] The text connected with a picture also plays an important role. Within certain limits it can guide eye movement and the period of fixation.[52]

Whether and how the perceived information is processed depends on the attitude of the viewer. Thus, Salomon takes up the concept of flexible allocation of cognitive resources and calls it 'amount of invested mental effort' (AIME).[53] He thinks that school children and students consider television a medium to be understood easily, a medium whose reception requires very little mental effort. From this judgement it can be concluded that test persons learned less from television programmes than from the corresponding print media. Viewer attitude also varied with specific types of programmes (e.g. news) or with experimentally induced attitudes towards watching television. If a person made a mental effort because of special instructions or because of a special programme, he/she remembered more of television programmes.[54]

This concept can also explain why, for example, studies of the remembering of television news only lead to values between 5 per cent and 25 per cent of the news.[55] Possibly viewers think that the processing of news does not require much mental effort, producing an effect called *Wissensillusion* (the illusion of knowledge).[56] People think themselves to be sufficiently informed, but actually they do not remember much.

Even if there are only few investigations in this field, the results mentioned above show that viewers know how to deal adequately with information explosion. In the course of their television socialization they develop visual schemes from audio-visual material that they view often. These schemes make recognition much more easy. Furthermore, they are able to vary their mental effort necessary for understanding (again we find the flexible allocation of cognitive resources mentioned above). The result can be a low valuation of the medium and as a consequence a low level of facts remembered (*Wissensillusion*).

Finally, it must not be forgotten that the viewer has the possibility to switch to a different channel or to switch off the set in case of inundation by information. Generally this phenomenon is described by the term 'gratification discrepancy'. The programme does not meet expectations – with regard to content and/or to form.[57] The continuous comparison of expected and obtained gratifications leads to evaluations which are related to the programme, the channel and the medium.[58] At short notice viewers selectively use this effect in the form of so-called 'mood-management'. 'Mood management' involves the use of programmes to satisfy subjective mental states. For instance, if a person is in a bad mood, because he/she is under pressure, and wants to change this, he/she will prefer to watch programmes which are relaxing and entertaining, such as nature films or comedies and game-shows.[59] In the long term such evaluations take effect in renewed processes of selection.[60] Programmes or channels which show a type and amount of information inadequate for the viewer who is doing the selecting, will not be switched on any more.

Thus, we discover that the viewer is not passively exposed to an information explosion on television – whether with respect to the selection of the channel and the visual perception or with regard to the processing and evaluation of information perceived. On the contrary, he/she uses intentionally – and by the flexible allocation of cognitive resources – the possibilities of gratification of the medium. If he/she has enough or is bored, they will change the channel or the activity. The cognitive activity of 'watching television' is far from a passive process of assimilating amounts of information, which are at best occasionally considered to be adequate; on the contrary, it is a process of selecting and processing, controlled to a great extent by the individual.

From memory to evaluation: results of research on television news

This general conclusion will now be illustrated by using the example of the reception of news, because news programmes are considered to be a very important television genre in Western democracies. They are thought to be the basis of uncensored political discussion and a prerequisite for the political activities of citizens. It is, accordingly, important that they are used by citizens in an appropriate way.

Empirical research pursues this idea of television news in so far as one of its main topics deals with the remembering of news. But the results achieved in about twenty years of research are not very promising. In general, viewers of news programmes regard themselves as well informed: in fact they remember – depending on the study – only between 5 per cent and 25 per cent of the news.

On the other hand, these values can be improved by an optimal arrangement of news: for example, by texts formulated in a colloquial and simple language, by pictures which fit with the content and which are not too emotionalized (cause-and-effect-pictures, curves), by the use of heads and summaries and by a moderate pace of news programmes.[61] Nevertheless, the impact of these factors should not be overestimated. A German researcher reckons that only 5 per cent of the performances of remembering can be influenced in this way. Some investigations put this higher at up to 10 per cent.[62]

Results on the question of whether viewers adjust their personal behaviour to the news are even more disillusioning. In American studies the people surveyed said that the news does not have much in common with their private life.[63] Moreover, between 40 per cent and 50 per cent watch the news for completely different motives: they regard news as entertaining, convenient, relaxing and cheaper than other activities. This finding fits with other results according to which people like to watch bad news up to 33 per cent more than good news.[64]

Considering these motives (which normative theories of news do not take seriously) the terrible scores in remembering television news are not so surprising. For a person who wants to get excited or wants to relax, to be entertained or to occupy himself with news, it is not necessary to perceive, understand, remember or incorporate everything in his repertoire of behaviour. If under these circumstances something is learned at all, it is learned at best casually. American researchers summarize the results as follows: 'Network news may be fascinating. It may be highly entertaining. But it is simply not informative.'[65]

But this summary is only partially correct. To be more precise, viewers with a much better understanding and a profounder processing of news show identifiable sociological and psychological characteristics. News is remembered especially well by viewers who are intelligent, better educated and politically aware and who regard television as a source of information to be taken seriously, who have a great interest in and a great knowledge of the respective issues and who talk and think about what they see on television. These persons can achieve scores of remembering of about 60 per cent or 70 per cent.

This result leads us to another relevant topic of research. American researchers discovered by empirical investigations that people from higher social classes were informed earlier and better about political and other issues than people from lower social classes.[66] This research generated the 'knowledge-gap' hypothesis. In subsequent investigations this 'knowledge-gap' effect was found particularly with respect to issues of national politics; it was less apparent in local and regional issues. Other factors exerting an important influence are general political awareness, interest in a specific issue or personal communication. Finally, types of knowledge are distributed in a different way amongst social classes: knowledge of facts is found more often in lower classes than knowledge about structures and broader developments. To summarize: the knowledge gap can be found especially with regard to structural knowledge about current issues of national politics. This phenomenon has been referred to as the 'communication effects gap', which comprises use, reception and application of information.

It would be a lesser evil if the socially different use of news programmes led only to a reinforcement of an already existing deficit in knowledge. However, the situation is worse because low scores in tests of remembering need not necessarily mean that the reception of news will be without consequences. A first emotional reaction and a superficial processing have to take place in any case. This phenomenon is highlighted in the 'cultivation of beliefs' approach of the American media researcher George Gerbner.[67] In his view, television has become a central instance of socialization for society. Correspondingly, the effects of television consist less in the transmission of specific information than in the cultivation of basic attitudes towards social reality.

The basic paradigm of Gerbner's empirical research is always a content analysis of television programmes with regard to manner and frequency of the occurrence of certain groups of persons, events or behaviour patterns. This content analysis is compared with existing characteristics of the so-called real world, thus providing a differentiation between the so-called world of television and the so-called real world. With respect to this distinction first-order beliefs and second-order beliefs can be distinguished. The former are an estimation of the frequencies attached to certain events and groups of persons (for example, the percentage of violent crimes in a society); the latter are generalized public opinions (for example: that politicians are not interested in the problems of the average citizen). Finally, viewers are asked to evaluate these beliefs. People who watch television often are expected to give answers which fit with the television world.

An example is taking extensive content analyses of presentation of violence as a starting point. Gerbner assumes that especially people who watch television often (who expose themselves to presentations of violence more often than other groups of viewers) consider the real world to be menacing. He says that he found out in different investigations that more people who watch television often than people who do not watch television so frequently are afraid of walking through the city at night, protect themselves from crime by weapons, dogs and locks, consider the worldwide political situation as constantly aggravating and the birth of children as irresponsible. The sum of these opinions is what Gerbner calls the scary world of people who watch television often.

These results were soon challenged.[68] Fortunately, the controversy led to a very productive discussion so that only a few years later numerous further studies on different topics – attitudes towards doctors, elderly people, the justice system, perception of wealth etc. – were produced, supporting the effects of the cultivation of beliefs.[69] Thus, people who watch television often, compared to people who do not use the medium to such a great extent, trust medicine, police, military, the educational system, organized religion, the press, television and the trade unions much more. On the other hand, they mistrust big companies and science. Furthermore, they overestimate the frequency of certain professional groups (doctors, lawyers, businessmen) in society as well as the frequency of divorces and prison sentences and of certain diseases. But multi-variable analyses show comparatively low influence of the sheer time that people watch television (between 1 and 6 per cent), whereas for example education has a much bigger influence on the estimations mentioned above.

In research accompanying a project concerning news for children (ZDF/LOGO) we asked for the children's first- and second-order beliefs with regard to their own living space as well as with regard to Germany in general. This approximately corresponds to Schütz's division into a 'world of actual reach' and a 'world of potential reach'. We consider this an effect which is called in literature 'the grass is greener in my own yard' effect. With regard to one's own living space estimations of the frequency of violent crimes, professional politicians, unemployed adolescents, diseased trees and AIDS sufferers are less menacing than with regard to Germany as a whole. Here we found that people considered the rate of violent crimes 25 times higher than it really was and the number of AIDS sufferers was overestimated 100 times. Furthermore, it turned out that especially children who were underprivileged in terms of education and opportunities, and who watch a lot of news and information programmes in a not very intensive way, considered the Federal Republic of Germany much more negatively than other groups.[70]

With regard to the influence of television on political attitudes the so-called 'video-malaise' hypothesis was formulated. According to this hypothesis, groups using exclusively television as a source of political information have a much more cynical attitude towards politics and politicians. This effect can be found primarily in households whose members do not read much, but have a lot of confidence in the medium that they use for entertainment. Results of the research from Germany show that the more entertainment is used, the more entertainingly politics is presented, the more probable is disillusionment with, and opting-out of, politics. The general 'video-malaise' thus turns into the more specific 'entertainment-malaise'.[71]

In order to anticipate future developments it is necessary to look at the changes that are influencing the medium and the genre at present. In the mid-1980s the news business in the United States has changed in a revolutionary manner because of buy-outs and takeovers. There is now no room left for socially meritorious, but less profitable news programmes. Even news programmes now have to earn more money than they cost. The audience of primetime news has become the target group of marketing departments. There is not much room left for a quiet and objective presentation of information. A political statement of an American politician in the news which lasted about 50 seconds in 1968 lasted only about 10 seconds in 1988.[72] Extreme examples such as 'Eyewitness News' and 'Action News' in New York, Los Angeles and Chicago have developed from these changes of conventional news programmes.[73] In the meantime the following news factors can be identified:

1. The story has to be oriented towards individuals or it must be possible to make it individual-oriented.
2. The story has to be dramatic and conflict-ridden, and at best contain violence.
3. The story has to contain 'action-elements' or at least events that can be observed.
4. The story has to be new and/or has to deviate from the familiar.[74]

In Germany circumstances are not yet as described above, but similar tendencies can be observed. An analysis on behalf of the Konrad-Adenauer-Stiftung carried out in 1992 showed that the news programmes of the public-service channels reserve the greatest part for the field of politics. For example, 60 per cent of the news of the first television channel, ARD, deals with German politics. The amount of statements by politicians compared to all quotations and speeches is at 60 per cent much higher than their share in the private commercial channels' news programmes (in RTL 45 per cent). The share of apolitical contributions is only about 14 per cent in ARD news and 21 per cent in ZDF news. Commercial channels like RTL and SAT 1 dedicate nearly 30 per cent of all contributions to so-called topics of human interest such as catastrophes or accidents, and also to positive events in the fields of culture, society and sports. The private channels report on crime much more often, in more detail and more prominently. There is also a tendency towards a more extensive and more cruel presentation of violence: crimes and accidents are shown more often. This approach represents a convergence with the popular press. But a trend towards an increased reporting on negative aspects can be found in several studies.[75] It can be assumed that these developments will not decrease.

Thus we find that the general and the media-specific psychological results on the question of information strain are also confirmed in the special field of news reception. In the face of a deluge of information the human being does not prove to be a viewer under strain, endangered by stress and infarct. On the contrary, he actively selects news programmes as a whole as well as items of information according to his specific interests. But we find that the motives and the effects involved, and underlying the reception of news, do not always correspond to normative theories of news. As the results concerning the knowledge gap show, more intelligent, formally better educated people from higher social classes in general approach news programmes with a different previous knowledge and a different attitude towards reception than people from lower social classes. Therefore, they are informed earlier and better about political, economic and medical issues than those from lower social classes and people who do not have such a good formal education. The information will be checked in detail according to subjective relevance and will be assimilated – or forgotten. By comparison, socially underprivileged groups regard the field of national politics (if they take note of it at all) presumably as a remote, dangerous, but quite entertaining world, which they experience – in the sense of the 'video-malaise' hypothesis and the cultivation hypothesis – as terrifying and threatening. A 'media class society' begins to take shape. The citizen who is competent for dealing with information has an amount of information at her/his disposal never before experienced in history. However, the process of dealing with it has to be learned. Groups with a good formal education and from higher social classes have a big advantage in this respect. For the communicatively incompetent recipient news programmes increasingly offer an overabundance of sensation-seeking pictures, which he/she processes only superficially and with a 'scary world attitude'. He becomes an apolitical 'chronic know-nothing'.[76] In this way a society could develop in which individual and collective possibilities of happiness will depend decisively on possessing the appropriate skills for dealing with information.

The competent viewer: moral standards for using the media as an alternative?

Let us summarize the conclusions so far. We found, on the one hand, that the human being has only limited cognitive capacities at her/his disposal and, on the other, that he/she uses them in an economic and flexible way. The exceptional situations are those in which he/she is confronted by an information explosion that is more than her/his capacities can cope with, that at the same time cannot be avoided and that then lead to strain, stress and infarct. These general results are also confirmed by the analysis of the processing of information while watching television. The viewer uses her/his cognitive capacities selectively and flexibly. Even in selecting the programme it turns out that the individual is not overwhelmed by a vast offering of television, but that he/she selects programmes likely to be appropriate with the help of variable search strategies according to needs, expectations and previous experiences of watching television. The viewer does not sit in front of the television set almost mesmerized, like the rabbit in front of the snake, let alone give it undivided attention. On the contrary, contact rates can be found which differ according to culture, programme and individual. Attitudes, expectations and previous knowledge play an important role, especially in the reception of news programmes.

At the same time not all individual strategies for selecting channels and programmes are adequate with regard to society and politics. The results of the 'communication effect gap' hypothesis, the 'cultivation' hypothesis and the 'entertainment' hypothesis indicate that an active, selective and intelligent handling of television can yield a substantial benefit. But it seems that not all sections of the population have the same competence for dealing with the media at their disposal.

Given such individual influences, one could argue that the viewer has to make sure her/himself that he/she has the greatest benefit from television by an appropriate previous knowledge, developing adequate motives for its use and adopting the right strategy for selecting channels and programmes. Thus, in this volume Lübbe identifies suitable moral standards for using the media: in effect he argues for a new ethics for using the media. In his view, moral standards for using the media are one of the most important elements of culture, on which the individual depends for her/his life style.

From the point of view of psychology Lübbe's argument is not wrong, because – among other things – its results concerning the flexible allocation of resources, concerning the amount of invested mental effort, and concerning the interest in issues, showed that individual attitudes strongly influence whether and how the consumption of television affects people. In this respect the viewer certainly has the liberty and the responsibility to expose her/himself only to such programmes whose assumed or actual effects he/she wishes or at least approves of for her/himself or for others. Furthermore, studies of the effects of teaching programmes of 'media literacy' show that individual proficiency in dealing 'appropriately' with television can be promoted by pedagogic means.[77] Children who took part in the respective teaching units were afterwards better able to identify the formal means of television production, could more easily differentiate between real and fictitious information, and were able to use their mental effort more variably while watching television than children who did not participate in the programmes.[78] Careful dealing with the media in the family – especially the explanation and ethical evaluation of contents – has similar effects.[79] Children from families which provide such explanation and ethical evaluation not only deal more selectively with television as a whole and with single genres (like for example advertisements); they also have a better political and geographical knowledge, less prejudices and fewer fears, are less aggressive and so on.[80]

Convincing as the claim for moral standards in using the media may be, the argument is problematic because it makes only the individual (and her/his educators) responsible for all the various effects produced by the media. If – for example – too much violence in the media leads to an increase in real violence, the viewer is made the responsible party by this argument, since he/she – because of a lack of decent morals – watched these programmes.[81] The producer, the actor, the programme director – they are relieved from responsibility, just as are the politicians and the lawyers concerned with the media. Lübbe argues in his chapter that suitable moral standards for using the media are culturally more important than good moral standards with regard to the media. This argument seems to be merely a new variation on a principle which can often be met in public debate on media questions: the others are to blame for undesirable effects of the media.

The following question has to be answered: is the viewer able to deal sensibly with the permanently increasing amount of information? From a micro-analytical point of view related only to the experience and the survival of the individual we answered this question positively, referring to varied strategies for selecting and coping. But, at the same time, we realized that not all strategies that are individually successful are sensible with regard to politics and society. With the public interest in mind it is essential to publicly formulate new moral standards for the media and to firmly fix these standards in the mind of the individual. In order to ensure that these public moral standards are not simply reduced to a rhetorical and symbolic role, without practical consequences, it is crucial to conduct an open public debate in the future about the appropriate political, economic and legal framework for the European media. The public-interest requirements are the subject of the chapter by Hoffmann-Riem which follows.

References

1. Deutsche Forschungsgemeinschaft, *Medienwirkungsforschung in der Bundesrepublik Deutschland*. Teil I: *Berichte und Empfehlungen*, Weinheim: VCH, 1986; P. Glotz, 'Chancen und Gefahren der Telekratie. Der Wandel der Kommunikationskultur seit 1984', *Die Neue Gesellschaft – Frankfurter Hefte 1* (1995), pp. 32–41; M. Jäckel, 'Auf dem Weg zur Informationsgesellschaft? Informationsverhalten und die Folgen der Informationskonkurrenz' in M. Jäckel and P. Winterhoff-Spurk (eds), *Politik und Medien: Analysen zur Entwicklung der politischen Kommunikation*, Berlin: Vistas, 1994, pp. 11–34; D. Stolte, 'Fernsehen heute: . . . oder Das Erbe des Archimedes' in H. Hoffmann (ed.), *Gestern begann die Zukunft*, Darmstadt: Wissenschaftliche Buchgesellschaft, 1994, pp. 88–105.

2. Media Perspektiven Basisdaten, *Daten zur Mediensituation in Deutschland 1993*, Frankfurt, 1993.

3. Media Perspektiven Basisdaten, 1993; B. Frank and H. Gerhard, 'Angebot und Nutzung von Fernsehprogrammen', *Media Perspektiven* 10 (1993), pp. 471–8.

4. Media Perspektiven Basisdaten, 1993; and B. Franzmann and D. Löffler, 'Leseverhalten in Deutschland 1992/93. Ergebnisse der ersten Repräsentativstudie zur Lage der lesenden Nation', *Media Perspektiven* 10 (1993), pp. 454–64.

5. See respectively N. Postman, 'Wir informieren uns zu Tode', *Die Zeit*, 2 October 1992, pp. 61–2; W. Kroeber-Riehl, *Bildkommunikation*, Munich: Vahlen, 1993; S. Baier, 'Der Informationsinfarkt', *Psychologie heute* 12 (1991), pp. 28–30.

6. P. Winterhoff-Spurk (ed.), *Psychology of Media in Europe – The State of the Art, Perspectives for the Future*, Leverkusen: Westdeutscher Verlag, 1995.

7. W. Tack, 'Das Gehirn als Computer. Der Mensch – ein informationsverarbeitendes Wesen' in H. Scheidgen, P. Strittmatter and W. Tack (eds), *Information ist noch kein Wissen*, Weinheim: Beltz, 1990, pp. 21–36.

8. D. W. Massaro and N. Cowan, 'Information processing models: microscopes of the mind', *Annual Review of Psychology* 44 (1993), pp. 383–425.

9. J. A. Anderson, *Kognitive Psychologie*, Heidelberg: Spektrum, 1988; M. H. Ashcraft, *Human Memory and Cognition*, Glenview, IL: Scott, Foresman & Company, 1989; M. W. Eysenck and M. T. Keane, *Cognitive Psychology: A Student's Handbook*, Hillsdale, NJ: Erlbaum, 1990; M. G. Wessels, *Kognitive Psychologie*, New York: Harper & Row, 1984.

10. O. Lanc, *Ergonomie*, Stuttgart: Kohlhammer, 1975.

11. P. Winterhoff-Spurk, 'Zum Zusammenhang von Blickbewegungen und

sprachlich-kognitiven Prozessen – ein Überblick', *Psychologische Rundschau* 31(4) (1980), pp. 261–76.

12. H. Engelkamp, *Das menschliche Gedächtnis. Das Erinnern von Sprache, Bildern und Handlungen*, Göttingen: Hogrefe, 1990; and W. Kintsch, *Gedächtnis und Kognition*, Berlin: Springer, 1982.

13. F. I. Craik and R. S. Lockhart, 'Levels of processing: a framework for memory research', *Journal of Verbal Learning and Verbal Behavior* 11 (1972), pp. 671–84; Eysenck and Keane, *Cognitive Psychology*; Wessels, *Kognitive Psychologie*.

14. R. N. Shepard, 'Recognition memory for words, sentences, and pictures', *Journal of Verbal Learning and Verbal Behavior* 6 (1967), pp. 156–63.

15. L. Standing, 'Learning 10,000 pictures', *Quarterly Journal of Experimental Psychology* 25 (1973), pp. 207–22.

16. S. T. Fiske, 'Social cognition and social perception', *Annual Review of Psychology* 44 (1993), pp. 155–94; and Wessels, *Kognitive Psychologie*.

17. Eysenck and Keane, *Cognitive Psychology*.

18. M. R. Banaji and D. A. Prentice, 'The self in social contexts', *Annual Review of Psychology* 45 (1994), pp. 297–332.

19. N. Semmer, 'Stress' in R. Asanger and G. Wenninger (eds), *Handwörterbuch Psychologie*, Weinheim: Psychologie Verlags Union, 1988, pp. 744–52.

20. C. Schneiderbauer, *Faktoren der Fernsehprogrammauswahl. Eine Analyse des Programminformationsverhaltens der Fernsehzuschauer*, Kommunikationswissenschaftliche Studien Band 13, Nuremberg: Verlag der Kommunikationswissenschaftlichen Forschungsvereinigung, 1991; and P. Winterhoff-Spurk, 'Wer die Wahl hat . . . – Medienpsychologische Aspekte der Fernsehprogrammvermehrung' in M. Jäckel and M. Schenk (eds), *Kabelfernsehen in Deutschland. Pilotprojekte, Programmvermehrung, private Konkurrenz, Ergebnisse und Perspektiven*, Munich: Fischer, 1991, pp. 159–80.

21. Compare B. Büchner, *Der Kampf um die Zuschauer. Neue Modelle zur Fernsehprogrammauswahl*, Munich: Fischer, 1989; J. Doll and U. Hasebrink, 'Zum Einfluss von Einstellungen auf die Auswahl von Fernsehsendungen' in J. Groebel and P. Winterhoff-Spurk (eds), *Empirische Medienpsychologie*, Munich: PVU, 1989, pp. 45–63; W. Donsbach, 'Selektive Zuwendung zu Medieninhalten. Einflussfaktoren auf die Auswahlentscheidung der Rezipienten', *Kölner Zeitschrift für Soziologie und Sozialpsychologie*, Sonderheft 30, 1989, pp. 392–405; M. Schenk, *Medienwirkungsforschung*, Tübingen: Mohr, 1987; and P. Vitouch, *Fernsehen und Angstbewältigung*, Opladen: Westdeutscher Verlag, 1993.

22. D. F. Roberts and C. M. Bachen, 'Mass communication effects', *Annual Review of Psychology* 32 (1981), pp. 307–56.

23. Compare surveys by Büchner, *Der Kampf um die Zuschauer*; M. Jäckel, 'Mediennutzung als Niedrigkostensituation', *Medienpsychologie* 4 (1992), pp. 246–66; and Schneiderbauer, *Faktoren der Fernsehprogrammauswahl*.
24. Compare P. Barwise and A. Ehrenberg, *Television and Its Audience*, London: Sage, 1988; G. J. Goodhart, A. S. C. Ehrenberg and M. A. Collins, *The Television Audience: Patterns of Viewing*, 2nd edn, Westmead: Saxon House, 1987; and M. Wober, *The Use and Abuse of Television: A Social Psychological Analysis of the Changing Screen*, Hillsdale, NJ: Erlbaum, 1988.
25. Barwise and Ehrenberg, *Television and Its Audience*.
26. Compare Büchner, *Der Kampf um die Zuschauer*; and B. Hurrelmann, H. Possberg and K. Nowitzky, *Familie und Erweitertes Medienangebot*, Düsseldorf: Begleitforschung des Landes Nordrhein-Westfalen zum Kabelpilotprojekt Dortmund, 1988.
27. Winterhoff-Spurk, 'Wer die Wahl hat . . . '.
28. B. S. Greenberg, R. Srigley, T. F. Baldwin and C. Heeter, 'Free system-specific cable guides as an incentive' in C. Heeter and B. S. Greenberg (eds), *Cable Viewing*, Norwood, NJ: Ablex, 1988, pp. 264–88.
29. C. Heeter and B. S. Greenberg, 'Profiling the zappers' in Heeter and Greenberg (eds), *Cable Viewing*, pp. 67–73.
30. Compare O. Hagemann, K. Renckstorf and H. D. Schröder, *Das Fernsehprogramm in Programmzeitschriften und Tageszeitungen. Ergebnisse einer Inhaltsanalytischen Untersuchung*, ZDF Schriftenreihe Medienforschung, Heft 34, 1986; M. H. Fischer, 'Die Rolle der Programmzeitschrift für das Einschaltverhalten beim Fernsehen', *Media Perspektiven* 9 (1983), pp. 577–83; M. Jäckel, 'Kabelfernsehen – ein einleitender Überblick' in Jäckel and Schenk (eds), *Kabelfernsehen in Deutschland*, pp. 9–29; and RSG Marketing Research, *ARD/ZDF – Kulturstudie. Repräsentative Bevölkerungsumfrage im Frühjahr/ Sommer 1989*, unpublished research report, Düsseldorf, 1990.
31. RSG Marketing Research, *ARD/ZDF – Kulturstudie*; Hagemann et al., *Das Fernsehprogramm in Programmzeitschriften und Tageszeitungen*; Schneiderbauer, *Faktoren der Fernsehprogrammauswahl*.
32. Enigma-Institut, *Akzeptanz des bayerischen Fernsehens*, unpublished volume of tables, Wiesbaden, 1991.
33. C. Heeter, 'The choice process model' in Heeter and Greenberg (eds), *Cable Viewing*, pp. 11–32.
34. Heeter, 'The choice process model'.
35. J. W. Payne, 'Contingent decision behavior', *Psychological Bulletin* 92(2) (1982), pp. 382–402.
36. W. R. Neuman, 'Programming diversity and the future of television: an empty cornucopia?' in S. Oskamp (ed.), *Television as a Social Issue*, Newbury Park: Sage, 1988, pp. 346–9.
37. D. R. Anderson and D. E. Field, 'Die Aufmerksamkeit des Kindes beim

Fernsehen: Folgerungen für die Programmproduktion' in M. Meyer (ed.), *Wie verstehen Kinder Fernsehprogramme?*, Munich: Saur, 1984, pp. 52–92.

38. B. Gunter, *Poor Reception*, Hillsdale, NJ: Erlbaum, 1987.

39. F. Brenne, *Zur Messung der Wirkung von Fernsehsendungen (II). Verbale Kommunikation unter dem Einfluss des Fernsehens*, unpublished research report of the Hans-Bredow-Institut, Hamburg, 1977.

40. D. R. Anderson, D. E. Field, P. A. Collins, E. P. Lorch and J. G. Nathan, 'Estimates of young children's time with television: a methodological comparison of parents' reports with timelapse video home observation', *Child Development* 56 (1985), pp. 1345–57.

41. J. Condry, *The Psychology of Television*, Hillsdale, NJ: Erlbaum, 1989.

42. M. R. Levy, 'The audience experience with television news', *Journalism Monographs* 55 (1978).

43. J. Stauffer, R. Frost and W. Rybolt, 'The attention factor in recalling network television news', *Journal of Communication* 33(1) (1983), pp. 29–37.

44. R. B. Bechtel, C. Achelpohl and R. Akers, 'Correlates between observed behavior and questionnaire responses on television viewing' in E. A. Rubinstein, G. A. Comstock and J. P. Murray (eds), *Television and Social Behavior*. Vol. IV: *Television in Day-to-day Life: Patterns of Use*, Rockville, MD: National Institute of Mental Health, 1972, pp. 274–344.

45. R. Kubey and M. Csikszentmihalyi, *Television and the Quality of Life*, Hillsdale, NJ: Erlbaum, 1990.

46. Heeter and Greenberg, *Cable Viewing*.

47. Heeter and Greenberg, 'Profiling the zappers'.

48. B. Keitz, *Wirksame Fernsehwerbung*, Würzburg: Physica, 1983; W. Kroeber-Riehl, 'Informationsüberlastung durch Massenmedien und Werbung in Deutschland. Messung-Interpretation-Folgen', *Die Betriebswirtschaft* 47(3) (1987), pp. 257–64.

49. B. Flagg, 'Children and television: effects of stimulus repetition on eye activity' in J. W. Senders, D. F. Fisher and R. A. Monty (eds), *Eye Movements and the Higher Psychological Functions*, Hillsdale, NJ: Erlbaum, 1978, pp. 279–92.

50. Kroeber-Riehl, *Bildkommunikation*, p. 60.

51. B. Bürkle, 'Zur schemageleiteten Rezeption von Fernsehnachrichten', unpublished diploma dissertation, Mannheim, 1985.

52. Winterhoff, 'Zum Zusammenhang von Blickbewegungen und sprachlich-kognitiven Prozessen'; P. Winterhoff-Spurk and R. Schmitt, 'Texte bei der Fernsehwerbung. Eine experimentelle Untersuchung zur Wirkung von Texten auf die Bildrezeption und die Bewertung von Werbespots', *Media Perspektiven* 2 (1985), pp. 142–47.

53. G. Salomon, 'Television watching and mental effort: a social psycho-

logical view' in J. Bryant and D. R. Anderson (eds), *Children's Understanding of Television*, New York: Academic, 1983, pp. 181–98.

54. B. Weidenmann, 'Der mentale Aufwand beim Fernsehen' in J. Groebel and P. Winterhoff-Spurk (eds), *Empirische Medienpsychologie*, Munich: PVU, 1989, pp. 134–49.

55. Gunter, *Poor Reception*; J. E. Newhagen, 'The evening's bad news: effects of compelling negative television news images on memory', *Journal of Communication* 42(2) (1992), pp. 25–41; and P. Winterhoff-Spurk, 'Perspektiven der Medienpsychologie', *Heidelberger Jahrbücher* 35, Heidelberg: Springer, 1991, pp. 67–82.

56. E. Noelle-Neumann, 'Lesen in der Informationsgesellschaft', *Gutenberg-Jahrbuch* 61, Mainz: Gutenberg-Gesellschaft, 1986, pp. 295–301.

57. Büchner, *Der Kampf um die Zuschauer*.

58. S. Deimling, J. Bortz and G. Gmel, 'Zur Glaubwürdigkeit von Fernsehanstalten', *Medienpsychologie* 3 (1993), pp. 203–19.

59. D. Zillman, 'Mood management: using entertainment to full advantage' in L. Donohew, H. E. Sypher and E. T. Higgins (eds), *Communication, Social Cognition, and Affect*, Hillsdale, NJ: Erlbaum, 1988, pp. 147–72; B. Schmitz and U. Lewandrowski, 'Trägt das Fernsehen zur Regulierung von Stimmungen bei?', *Medienpsychologie* 1 (1993), pp. 64–84.

60. Schenk, *Medienwirkungsforschung*; M. Schenk and P. Rössler, 'Rezipientenorientierter Programmvergleich: Ein brauchbares Modell für die Fernsehforschung?', *Media Perspektiven* 12 (1990), pp. 785–791.

61. Gunter, *Poor Reception*.

62. H. B. Brosius, 'Die Wirkung von Musik in Informationsfilmen', *Medienpsychologie* 1 (1990), pp. 144–55.

63. Stauffer, Frost and Rybolt, 'The attention factor in recalling network television news'; A. M. Rubin, 'Uses, gratifications, and media effects research' in J. Bryant and D. Zillmann (eds), *Perspectives on Media Effects*, Hillsdale, NJ: Erlbaum, 1986, pp. 281–301.

64. J. B. Haskins, 'The trouble with bad news', *Newspaper Research Journal* 2(2) (1981), pp. 3–16.

65. T. E. Patterson and R. D. McClure, *The Unseeing Eye: The Myth of Television Power in National Elections*, New York: Putnam, 1976.

66. P. J. Tichenor, G. A. Donohue and C. N. Olien, 'Mass media flow and differential growth in knowledge', *Public Opinion Quarterly* 34 (1970), pp. 159–70.

67. G. Gerbner, L. Gross, M. Morgan and N. Signorelli, 'Living with television: the dynamics of the cultivation process' in Bryant and Zillman (eds), *Perspectives on Media Effects*, pp. 17–40.

68. P. Hirsch, 'The "scary" world of the non-viewer and other anomalies: a reanalysis of Gerbner et al.'s findings on the cultivation hypothesis. Part I', *Communication Research* 7(4) (1980), pp. 403–56; P. Hirsch,

'On not learning from one's own mistakes. A reanalysis of Gerbner et al.'s findings on the cultivation hypothesis. Part II', *Communication Research* 8(1) (1981), pp. 3–37.

69. R. P. Hawkins and S. Pingree, 'Television's influence on social reality' in NIMH (ed.), *Television and Behavior: Ten Years of Scientific Progress and Implications for the Eighties*, Rockville, MD: NIMH, 1982, Vol. 2, pp. 224–47.

70. P. Winterhoff-Spurk, *Fernsehen und Weltwissen. Der Einfluss von Medien auf Zeit-, Raum- und Personenschemata*, Opladen: Westdeutscher Verlag, 1989.

71. C. Holtz-Bacha, 'Massenmedien und Politikvermittlung – Ist die Videomalaise-Hypothese ein adäquates Konzept?' in Jäckel and Winterhoff-Spurk (eds), *Politik und Medien*, pp. 181–91.

72. D. C. Hallin, 'Sound bite news: television coverage of elections, 1968–1988', *Journal of Communication* 42(2) (1992), pp. 5–24.

73. P. Winterhoff-Spurk, V. Heidinger and F. Schwab, *Reality-TV – Formate und Inhalte eines neuen Programmgenres*, Schriftenreihe der LAR, Band 3, Saarbrücken: Logos-Verlag, 1994.

74. R. J. Harris, *A Cognitive Psychology of Mass Communication*, Hillsdale, NJ: Erlbaum, 1989.

75. U. M. Krüger, '"Soft news" – kommerzielle Alternative zum Nachrichtenangebot öffentlichrechtlicher Rundfunkanstalten. SAT 1, RTL plus, ARD und ZDF im Vergleich', *Media Perspektiven* 6 (1985), pp. 479–90; and E. Sassmann and S. Wille, *Ein Nachrichtentag in Europa. Studie der Hörer- und Sehervertratung*, Teil 1 and 2. Vienna, 1991.

76. S. M. Lipset, *Political Man: The Social Bases of Politics*, New York: Doubleday, 1959.

77. D. R. Anderson, 'Televison literacy and the critical viewer' in Bryant and Anderson (eds), *Children's Understanding of Television*, pp. 297–330.

78. J. L. Singer and D. G. Singer, 'Implications of childhood television viewing for cognition, imagination, and emotion' in Bryant and Anderson (eds), *Children's Understanding of Televison*, pp. 265–96; A. Dorr, S. B. Graves and E. Phelps, 'Television literacy for young children', *Journal of Communication* 30(3) (1980), pp. 71–83.

79. R. J. Desmond, J. L. Singer and D. G. Singer, 'Family mediation: parental communication patterns and the influence of television on children' in J. Bryant (ed.), *Television and the American Family*, Hillsdale, NJ: Erlbaum, 1990.

80. Anderson, 'Television literacy and the critical viewer'; P. M. Greenfield, *Kinder und neue Medien. Die Wirkungen von Fernsehen, Videospielen und Computern*, Munich: PVU, 1987; J. Van Evra, *Television and Child Development*, Hillsdale, NJ: Erlbaum, 1990; Singer and Singer, 'Implications of childhood television viewing'; P. Winterhoff-Spurk,

Fernsehen. Psychologische Befunde zur Medienwirkung, Bern: Huber, 1986.

81. P. Winterhoff-Spurk, 'Spectateur ou acteur? Considérations psychologiques sur la violence médiatique', *Les Cahiers de la sécurité intérieure* 20 (1995), pp. 1–10.

6

Regulating for Cultural Standards: A Legal Perspective

WOLFGANG HOFFMANN-RIEM

It has become a part of contemporary tradition to view mass communication and the media in the context of certain social values, such as, for example, facilitating the individual development of citizens, encompassing also their socialization and enculturation. The media are, in short, essential to the processes of integration of the individual into society and of acquiring the cultural traditions of a society. Individual development in and through communication ranks as important not only for the workability of democracy, ensuring such fundamental values as freedom and diversity of expression. The ability to communicate and participation in communication are, at the same time, indispensable elements of a civilized state that values education, information and the arts. In addition, as society becomes increasingly complex, so communications media are ever more crucial in providing citizens with an adequate social and cultural perspective so that they can continue to make sense of society. They have a vital role in sustaining cultural identity and in realizing the values of social participation and cohesion. In short, there is a 'public interest' in communication. This public interest provides the goals of legal regulation of the media.

The public service idea of broadcasting as developed in Europe focuses on the role of broadcasting as mediator and participant in society's process of communication. This idea is also taken up in several European constitutions. Insofar as the state is entrusted with a special task in this way, the underlying conviction is that broadcasting's ability to realize public service values does not develop without external support, for example solely as the outcome of the functioning of market forces. One prominent European example of such a view is the judicial practice of Germany's Federal

Constitutional Court, which has attempted in numerous rulings to concretize the basic right of freedom of communication and of the media (Article 5 of the Basic Law) in such a way that the freedom of the communications system does not remain a legal fiction, but gains *de facto* significance for all citizens. The Federal Constitutional Court emphasizes that the regulation of the broadcasting order is a legislative task.[1] The state should not be allowed to intervene in the concrete activities of broadcasting on the programme side: rather, it must unconditionally respect journalistic independence. But it must design the structures of the broadcasting system in such a way that they remain effective with regard to the public interest tasks of the media.

In the opinion of the German Federal Constitutional Court, the freedom of opinion formation and of the media anchored as basic rights in the constitution extends beyond the freedom to express views and assert facts as a broadcaster and as a journalist, to disseminate them via the mass media or in any other form, and, for example, to exploit them commercially to one's own advantage. In addition, it is absolutely essential to ensure the freedom of recipients to inform and orient themselves individually and collectively with the help of communication services. Insofar as the realization of the freedom of opinion formation through the media is jeopardized, the state is called upon to put in place special safeguards. Protection is required, for example, against abusive activities aimed at gaining one-sided influence, whether issuing from the state or from private interests. Safeguards must also be provided to ensure that the mass media retain and improve their communication performance in the citizens' interests by reference to such principles as social responsibility, objectivity, diversity and cultural quality. Communication performance presupposes more than that the media employ new technological possibilities. The more burning issue from a societal and 'public interest' perspective is whether all the communication values that a modern media system can provide are effectively operationalized. It is by no means automatically guaranteed, for example, that the media can help tap the individual and collective potential in terms of creativity and innovation or that they can exploit and further disseminate society's stock of knowledge in its entire breadth. The growing market orientation of the media, especially broadcasting, leads to the risk that whole bodies of cultural experience will be submerged and that communication opportunities will remain untapped inasmuch as they cannot be commercially exploited.

Historically, the public service idea embodied in European broadcasting has a special model function in the field of audio-visual services as a guarantor of the protection of such values as freedom and diversity of expression. These values are open to development in the content of communication, adaptable to the particular cultural forms and socialization requirements of a society and to its technological and economic conditions. But it must be emphasized that such communication values remain the central point of reference for judging media performance not only in traditional broadcasting communication but in all forms of media communication which currently or potentially have an influence on the information level, and on the knowledge and outlook of the recipient, comparable to that traditionally exerted by the press and broadcasting media.[2]

Correspondingly, the law regulating media communication must be normatively adapted to the respective technological, economic, socio-cultural and political conditions in such a way that the *de facto* ability of the communicators to express their opinions and that of the recipients comprehensively to form their opinions without bias and without manipulation – in other words, 'freely' – are guaranteed. Insofar as forms of societal self-regulation (in particular, but not only, that of the market) prove insufficient in this respect, the state is called upon to provided regulation, whether through the creation of a legal framework to structure self-regulation ('regulated self-regulation') or through the direct regulation of the behaviour of the actors concerned.

Mass communication in a segmented and fragmented media market

In the meantime it is common knowledge that digitalization and compression technology are enabling a marked proliferation and greater differentiation of audio-visual products, new media (distribution) services, and an increase and diversification of service providers. The still evocative term 'multimedia' indicates the wealth of possibilities with this changed framework, for example as the result of a new distribution infrastructure, the use of new computer storage technologies, the transformation of pictures into computer-compatible symbolic languages or the integration of television and video functions into the computer. The multifunctional use of the traditional television set as a data-processing machine and as a medium of mass communication is becoming a technological reality. 'Global/national information infrastructure' and 'information super-highways' are just two of the catchphrases signposting the still unexploited development potential in this field.

Also becoming a technological reality is direct access to the content of audio-visual services, although in the case of mass communication only in the form of prepackaged programmes. Even so, possibilities for influencing dramaturgic development or camera perspective are no longer a utopian vision. In particular the field of virtual reality is opening up new directions of media development.

Emerging technological scenarios indicate a need for an appropriate response by media law. One argument is that the new opportunities for time management by recipients and the possibility of interactive influence in programme selection are producing the convergence of individual and mass communication – with the consequence that the regulation of the media (especially broadcasting) has been rendered by and large obsolete.[3] The economic market, it is claimed, suffices as a regulator.

Assessment of this thesis requires a recollection of previous rationales for regulation, which will be presented here with a special focus on (radio and television) broadcasting. Worldwide, and not least in Europe, broadcasting regulation by the state has never been solely justified by a scarcity of frequencies.[4] As a substantive justification in the future, as in the past, the fact remains that communication through mass media introduces constitutionally significant risks of a *de facto* 'unfree' expression and opinion formation. Special risks exist with respect to broadcasting consequent on its specific mode of production and reception as well as the nature of its financing structure – particularly the effects of advertising on programmes. In future, if anything a greater potential for influence on recipients can be expected rather than a reduction of manipulatory possibilities. Given the various experiences of market failure and the special potential for concentration of the media sector, it is unlikely that these risks will be avoided by means of the increase in services and perhaps even of media operators. It is equally unlikely that the character of the content of mass communication (and thereby the scope for mass influence) will erode as a consequence of any opportunities for individual recipients to gain access to, or even limited interactivity with, media.

Reference to 'mass' communication as a basis for justifying a special regulation of the media (i.e. to a form of communication addressed to an undifferentiated general audience) is based on the presumed significance and implied risks of such communication. Production for, and distribution to, the general public – regardless of how many members of society actually make use of these opportunities – gives rise to a form of communication whose structural context requires the special attention of the state.

Communication targeted at the 'masses' is characterized by special types of production and distribution which have content-related implications. Thus it is generally produced by companies which operate on a quasi-industrial basis. Elements of standardized mass production are not only to be found in the computer-controlled production methods of modern pop music and its use by the editorial teams of music-oriented format radio, but also in the assembly-line atmosphere of modern television soap opera productions or in the data-bank-linked development of jokes for talk shows and quiz programmes. In terms of content, the products consist to a considerable extent of the reproduction of previously successful models; they fall back upon stereotypes and standardized simplifications. There is no basis for the assumption that such mass-produced methods will be employed to a lesser extent in the more fragmented and segmented media market of the future. Indeed, expanding programme requirements will demand their increased use. Furthermore, in view of the scarcity of programme software there will be a temptation to maximize their value by re-using them almost endlessly as repeats as well as by exploiting them more fully in cinema, television, video and other product markets. What is more, they will be regularly rereleased by programme providers in order to capitalize on transmission rights. These forms of broadcasting use for mass markets will tend to increase in the foreseeable future.

Such quasi-industrial forms of production and distribution make it relatively easy to expand the number of programmes on offer. This process leads almost inevitably to confusion on the part of the recipients. Assistance in orienting oneself and selecting programmes in this more confused context is possible and will presumably be provided in future by specialist companies. In all probability, they will also include programme providers which are interlinked with companies from the broadcasting industry, so that mutual gains can be made. It is obvious that this sort of development in the media industry creates a potential for manipulation. The latter can already be seen *in statu nascendi* when flicking through programme guides, as they increasingly seek to offer selection tips. Also, computer programmes can be used to reconstruct the taste and preferences of respective recipients from their previous choice of programmes and, on this basis, work out individual programme recommendations and selections. The resultant newly 'transparent' and manipulable recipients can then be selectively confronted with, *inter alia*, advertising messages which take into account their individual characteristics, in the process also seeking quietly to guide their consumer behaviour. This phenomenon provides an example of how the new technologies can trigger new risks for freedom of expression.

By means of interactive demand recipients are less tied to a fixed-sequence viewing order, for instance by video on demand. In addition, albeit within narrow limits, the rigid role demarcation between communicator and recipient can be challenged with the help of interactive systems. But such possibilities do not eliminate the dependence of recipients on (mass) producers. They still remain, on the whole, restricted by the constraints of prefabricated programme content and by the technological specificities of the medium. The possible future increase in the freedom of choice for recipients will tend to relate in the foreseeable future to marginal rather than substantial aspects of media communication.

Justification for regulation by the state

Irrespective of the changes in the methods of production and distribution and the modes of reception, audio-visual mass communication will continue to retain its influence on information levels, perceptions of the world, and attitudes and outlooks of its recipients, and still decisively shape the process of opinion formation in society. The previous need for regulation will not be fundamentally changed, especially insofar as the traditional types of programmes on offer and forms of reception will in their essentials continue to exist and remain significant. They will be joined by new communication contents and forms, for which the need for regulation will have to be newly defined in each specific case. One risk that deserves special attention in this context is that already observable cleavages based on differences of knowledge and outlook will be compounded by new cleavages based on 'usage', and on varying technical and intellectual abilities to handle the new products and services (a topic taken up in Lübbe's chapter). As media competences are unevenly distributed in society (being for instance class- and age-specific), there are risks of a cultural class society. These risks are not eliminated merely by the availability of a larger number of products and services or by the possibility of an interactively controlled and time-shifting access of users to the programmes provided. Guaranteeing the freedom of expression and of opinion formation for citizens continues, in other words, to justify taking regulatory precautions to ensure the workability of a *de facto* free media system; its legal specification remains an indispensable requirement.

For the purpose of legal categorization it is important to note that audio-visual communication remains mass communication even if the individual contents (for instance films) are available on demand at any time or can be successively accessed (near video-on-demand). It has never been doubted, for example, that the newspaper is a mass medium even though it can be consumed in accordance with individual preferences at any time and competes with other publications for breakfast-table reading or though it may even be 'demanded' (read) a few days later. Whether and in what respect a need for regulation exists for mass media cannot be determined according to conceptual categorizations, but according to the particular characteristics of the medium and its potential for risk to the public interest. It is highly unlikely that this potential for risk will be eliminated by new developments. Hence it is inappropriate to delimit discussion about the need for regulation and its normative legitimation by reference to an inherited and narrow concept of broadcasting and to omit provision for any regulation outside the realm of traditional broadcasting. The need for regulation is not derived from static concepts such as that of 'broadcasting'. In functional terms, it also applies to so-called 'broadcasting-like' services which are replacing traditional broadcasting and extending its possibilities. At the same time it is important to respect the need for regulation to be specifically tailored to the discrete risk potential of individual media products and services. This potential is different in print media from, for example, audio-visual media, and perhaps different in broad- and narrow-cast programmes from an electronic video library.

Limits to effective regulation

But the main problem is not the justification of regulation as such but its specification and differentiation, something which must also take account of the factors conditioning the possibility of effective implementation. Throughout the world, broadcasting, especially market-oriented broadcasting, is only to a limited degree susceptible to effective regulation.[5] This insight applies even more in the case of a market for audio-visual communication which is even more fragmented and segmented. Regulatory and supervisory obstacles emerge, for example, as a result of the diversification of programme activities, the 'interlocking' of the various (often multimedia) companies operating in the media market, trans-national market structures, and expanding international operations.

The capacity for legal regulation is influenced by the structure of communication itself. One illustrative example is provided by a communication system such as the Internet. Although the Internet was not developed for mass communication, it is evolving in such a way that it can also distribute mass-communication services. Video films and the like can, for instance, be distributed via the Internet – albeit, up to now, with slow transmission speeds. Designed as the 'network of networks', the Internet was created with state assistance (from the US Defence Department and educational institutions). But it has meanwhile developed a 'spontaneously' self-regulating structure. In the face of such a structure a goal-oriented intervention by an external institution such as a state is bound to be by and large unsuccessful.

More promising from an implementation perspective are measures that seek self-regulation, and they stand the best chance of success if they work with structural targets instead of with concrete directives about behaviour. In this respect, due to its model function there is a great deal to learn from experience with the Internet for future developments in other fields of communication.

The success of media regulation and supervision is jeopardized not only if it fails appropriately to take into account the special technical characteristics of the respective media system. Above all, it is at risk if regulation clashes over a long period with the self-interests of the actors being regulated. In fact, business enterprises also have a certain interest in state regulation, for example as a means of creating a more stable framework for investment and of maintaining established structures – by preventing aggressive competition. But business enterprises only support such regulation insofar as its content is consistent with their own interests – a possibility which is facilitated by the neo-corporatist decision-making structures of modern democracies and which in some countries – for example, in Germany – has acquired an almost textbook quality through the astonishing proximity of some media enterprises to politics – and vice versa. This closeness of interests in the content of regulation limits the possibilities of effective intervention.

In this framework, however, the state can make use of the interest of business enterprises in limited regulation to urge the anchoring of conflicting public interests in media regulation. In particular, it can set an institutional framework for self-regulation – for example, for a market-delivered media communication supplemented by institutions of voluntary self-control and countervailing safeguards and the like. It can also institute a form of state supervision as a safety net, which can at least be tightened if self-regulation fails. But regulation will always constitute a difficult tightrope walk, since an excessively intensive regulation can suppress the freedom of expression and creative potential associated with private autonomy and self-interest, whereas regulation which is too weak threatens to become no more than a symbolic political measure.

Focal points for state regulation

The process of identifying in which fields – for the protection of which objects and on the grounds of which risks – state regulation is expedient or even imperative, and which instruments are appropriate in each case, requires a discriminating diagnosis of current developments and a prognosis of future developments, combined with the willingness to effect change and improvement in the case of misjudgements. A number of issue areas are outlined below as exemplifying the continuing need for regulation.

Regulation relating to concrete programme content will be just as difficult to justify in the future as in the present and the past. The basic problem of this type of media regulation is that it involves risks for the freedom of communication. Such regulation is most likely to be acceptable in terms of constitutional law if it serves to protect objects which enjoy general protection in the legal system. Hence the main limitations on freedom of communication come in the form of general laws rather than of media legislation itself: for instance, in the form of protection of personal reputation, protection against unfair competition, and protection of young people from damage to their development from, for instance, pornography or violence.[6] Such risks will not disappear in the multimedia era but will in all probability take on new forms.

Another type of regulation is represented by measures to protect the effective functioning of the communication system. If effective functioning is to be guaranteed in the sense of freedom for the recipient too (by prevention of bias, freedom from manipulation, diversity of content), it is no longer adequate to regulate the provision of broadcasting services solely by reference to the broadcasting institutions. This approach to regulation would neglect the effects on the contents of communication emanating from 'upstream' and 'downstream', for instance from production, the acquisition of rights, resale, and (advertising) financing. The influences, manipulation and the like occurring at these other levels are all the more difficult to encompass purely at the institutional level of broadcasting, given that the responsibility and *de facto* capacity for action of the 'broadcasters' is narrowing. An important aspect of this development is that broadcasting companies are to an increasing extent producing less themselves ('outsourcing') and have become more and more simply programme commissioning and distributing agencies with a correspondingly thinned-out 'editorial' responsibility (the publisher concept of broadcasting). Currently, observable market trends tend to confirm this picture.

But the process of division of labour in the media sector does not prevent a host of diagonal, vertical and horizontal links among companies involved in production, broadcasting, resale, etc. New types of linkages are becoming apparent, especially between the owners of transmission networks and the companies responsible for communication content. A look at the United States shows growing links of all kinds which can only be slowed down by the Federal Communications Commission: for example, between cable and telephone companies, programme production companies, copyright agencies, broadcasters, advertising companies and others. In Europe, too, such links will increase in the wake of the liberalization of the telecommunications sector, and new actors – in Germany, for example, at the moment the energy supply companies – are becoming active. Linkages of these kinds are a response not just to market opportunities but also to competitive risks. Particularly because there is a threat of new competition in the era of surplus capacity and growth in the communications branch, the already powerful firms have a special self-interest in limiting future competition, or at least in ensuring that its risks remain controllable. If the self-regulatory power of competition is to be maintained, it is simply not sufficient to work with general anti-trust law, since it is unable appropriately to avert media- and communications-specific risks.

A highly important form of regulation in future will be the guarantee of appropriate access (on the basis of the principle of equal opportunity) to the various levels of production, broadcasting, distribution and resale. Especially significant is the maintenance of open access to programme production and to programme acquisition, including access to copyright. If programme distributors such as broadcasters or cable companies, for example, have a (*de facto*) preferential access to programme production or to the rights market, their 'filtering' power will grow. This power, which also represents a power to exclude competitors, will strengthen if state regulation does not provide for a certain opening of access. First indications of regulations of this type can be found in the American Cable Television Consumer Protection and Competition Act of 1992.[7] The Act places a duty on vertically integrated companies to sell programme rights on equal terms even to competing broadcasters. This duty was, for example, a precondition in the United States for the satellite broadcasters Hughes and Hubbard before they 'dared' in 1994 to take up competition with established broadcasters. Access of broadcasters to the distribution network can also be ensured by state assistance, in the form of conditions (if need be, preferential prices) which support programme distribution by financially weaker but (in terms of the public service idea) important broadcasters. One approach, for example, is to make sure that carriage via the networks is structured on a common carrier basis, a construction which would probably not be sustainable in the long run in view of competing networks.[8] Possibly, however, a limited 'must-carry' obligation will be indispensable and sufficient. Without a corresponding legally supported ease of access to distribution technologies the main casualty will be culturally-oriented programmes, which do not cater for mass taste. The most likely survivors would be those programmes designed for cultural élites with high purchasing power.

Obstacles in the form of access problems can also develop for recipients (consumers). Apart from a right to non-discriminatory access, the regulatory framework must also include protection against excessive rates and being repeatedly 'forced' to buy new equipment to keep up with technological innovations (for instance, in the field of reception technology for digital television). In addition, provisions are needed for consumer protection and for rights to data protection. Ensuring access is part of the public interest in guaranteeing a 'basic provision' of communication/information services as part of the concept of universal service (note here Article 87 f. para. 1 of the German Basic Law). In comparison with the period of broadcasting and telecommunications monopolies which, for example, had numerous possibilities of internal cross-subsidization, this 'basic provision' can no longer be taken for granted in view of the differentiation of services and the market-oriented provision of infrastructure (with geographical and class-related differentiation of access). Media regulation is, accordingly, becoming increasingly enmeshed with regulation of consumer protection. In this new context it seems sensible to recommend the creation of institutions whose purpose is systematically to observe and evaluate services and programmes from the perspective of the recipient and which, on this basis, are able to develop information and education services for media consumers. Similar proposals (as for a *Stiftung Medientest*, a special foundation for media consumer information) have been put forward in Germany, for example, by the Weizsäcker Commission.[9] The involvement of media consumer organizations in regulatory decision-making processes, proposed by this Commission, also provides opportunities for an improved balancing of various interests – drawn not just from the media companies and the regulatory institutions but increasingly from the recipients.

Means of strengthening implementation capability

The mere creation of regulatory norms in the public interest does not on its own ensure their implementation. The variety of difficulties of norm implementation in the field of media regulation will not be dealt with in greater detail here.[10] It should be emphasized, however, that the articulation of normative goals can also serve to support and strengthen societal expectations, which in turn can facilitate the implementation of state regulation. Media enterprises which are successful in the market, and which seek to provide the advertising industry with an attractive and popular set of programmes, regularly react sensitively to public criticism or to threats to their image. Experience shows that media regulation and supervision are likely to be most active and effective if they can build on the support of other actors – for example, political office holders and also the general public – or if supervisory bodies can be forced by these actors to perform their tasks more effectively.

Ensuring the presence and effectiveness of critical public opinion is, accordingly, a major additional task of broadcasting supervision by the state. But societal control presupposes access to information about relevant company structures and their programme policies, etc. The interest of companies in the protection of their trade secrets must be set against the public interest in the effective control of those companies, given that they exert a powerful influence on public opinion and on the information levels and value systems of citizens. The legal system can and must, therefore, stipulate more transparency and provide supervisory bodies with more effective instruments to enforce the promotion of transparency.

Such considerations indicate that media regulation and supervision have to be restructured at a time of enormous increase in transmission capacities and contents and of a consequent confusion of service providers and programmes. The notion of a sovereign state regulating to implement a unitary public interest will probably prove unrealistic in this context: frustrated expectations would be pre-programmed (the 'overloading' of the state). But there are opportunities to establish regulatory structures composed of non-state actors which can make use of the self-interest of the various actors – including their interest in autonomy – in the framework of a concept of 'regulated self-regulation'. In this way expectations about the regulatory state can be reduced to the maintenance of responsibility for the framework and structure of the media system. The effectiveness of a (regulated) self-regulation in the media sector depends also on keeping open the public discourse about media and supporting the development of countervailing forces.

On safeguarding the public service idea

Within the regulatory framework there are various possible strategies for taking advantage of, or compensating for the disadvantages of, the coexistence and conflict of different structures: above all, ensuring and safeguarding a 'structural diversification' in the media system. One model for such a combination of different structures was and is the dual broadcasting system of public service broadcasting, on the one hand, and commercial broadcasting, on the other. The structurally-induced deficits of one 'pillar' of the dual order are supposed to be offset as far as possible by the other, just as the strengths of each are supposed to serve as incentives and yardsticks for the other. Journalistic competition is supposed to help in promoting diversity in news and current affairs broadcasting and a programme quality to complement this diversity. In this way public service broadcasting is supposed to and can set standards as a result of its considerable freedom from market-oriented financing and from the corresponding need to take into account advertising clients: it can also influence the recipients' expectations about commercial broadcasting.

But it remains questionable how long, or whether and how, this concept will remain viable in future. It rests on the continued existence of public service broadcasting, which, for its part, requires a statutory framework. Hence conditions need to be vouchsafed in which public service broadcasting not only is internally effective but also receives external political support. In the final analysis, it will only be able to secure this position by means of its programme performance. To this end, public service broadcasting will have to open itself further to the trend towards a target-group approach, in its general programmes as well as in special-interest programming, and develop new approaches to an increased individualization of media use by making use of interactivity.

The more fragmented and segmented the media structure becomes in future, the more differentiated will have to be the means of implementing the public service idea, including also in the field of commercial broadcasting. It will be crucial to ensure that the legal and moral obligations of commercial broadcasting, as well as of public service broadcasters, are defined not just on the basis of economic criteria and commercial calculations. If commercial broadcasters sacrifice public service attitudes in their search for revenue and profits, they will cease to be able to justify the privileged treatment that they now enjoy and to be able to defend it in the future. If society's communication needs remain unsatisfied by the services offered by market-oriented broadcasters, public service broadcasting is by no means automatically obliged to fill this gap. An example of a way in which this tendency might be counteracted would be the empowerment of regulators to skim off profits. These revenues could then be used as 'compensatory payments' to financially support the production of neglected programmes and their distribution by broadcasters.

Such a 'restructuring' will seem particularly attractive in the future when the task is to create culturally sophisticated productions (in the broadest sense) and ensure that they are distributed via broadcasting channels. Innovative approaches to programme production are particularly deserving of financial support, given that their commercial profitability is so uncertain that the companies operating in the market hesitate to make the necessary investments. If, with this objective in mind, steps are taken to skim off profits from those companies which subordinate public service values to commercial success, it must be guaranteed that the revenue is not channelled (unproductively in media terms) into the general state budget. Rather, it must be used to counteract deficiencies of content and quality in the communication system. The need for such counter-action is, of course, that much less pressing the more effective public service broadcasting remains. On the other hand, there is no sensible reason for limiting public service obligations solely to public service broadcasting and for exempting the commercial pillar of the broadcasting order from corresponding expectations.

Conclusion

The communication system of the future will experience a number of new forms of differentiation. In terms of programme content, this development includes, in a pluralistic society, acknowledging and working with heterogeneity and utilizing the innovative power that can be released by the juxtaposition of different interests and structures. The media law of the future should foster such an innovative power. But the legal system can only do this if on its own part it provides for its own learning capability. An appropriate legal regulation of broadcasting in the future requires, accordingly, a clear innovative thrust. The traditional instruments of media regulation have already often failed in the past and are only to a limited degree suitable when it comes to shaping the future.

References

1. Bundesverfassungsgericht, Ruling of 16 June 1981, *Entscheidungen des Bundesverfassungsgerichts*, vol. 57, Tübingen, 1982, pp. 295–335; and Bundesverfassungsgericht, Ruling of 4 November 1986, *Entscheidungen des Bundesverfassungsgerichts*, vol. 73, Tübingen, 1987, pp. 118–205.

2. W. Hoffmann-Riem, 'Kommunikations- und Medienfreiheit' in E. Benda, W. Maihofer and H.-J. Vogel (eds), *Handbuch des Verfassungsrechts der Bundesrepublik Deutschland*, 2nd edn, Berlin/New York: De Gruyter, 1994, pp. 191–262.

3. M. Bullinger, *Kommunikationsfreiheit im Strukturwandel der Telekommunikation*, Baden-Baden: Nomos Verlag, 1980.

4. Bundesverfassungsgericht, 1982; Hoffmann-Riem, 'Kommunikations- und Medienfreiheit'.

5. For an overview see W. Hoffmann-Riem, *Regulating Media: Licensing and Supervision of Broadcasting in Six Countries*, New York: Guilford Publications, 1995.

6. S. Ruck, 'Zur Unterscheidung von Ausgestaltungs- und Schrankengesetzen im Bereich der Rundfunkfreiheit', *Archiv des Öffentlichen Rechts* 117 (1992), pp. 543–66.

7. Federal Communications Commission, *Implementation of Section 19 of the Cable Television Consumer Protection and Competition Act 1992*, First Report, 19 September 1994, CS Docket No. 94–48.

8. E. Noam, 'Beyond liberalisation II. The impending doom of common carriage', *Telecommunications Policy* 18(6) (1994), pp. 435–52.

9. J. Groebel *et al.*, *Bericht zur Lage des Fernsehens*, Gütersloh: Verlag Bertelsmann Stiftung, 1995.

10. Hoffmann-Riem, *Regulating Media*, 1995.

7

Nothing Can Replace Reading

WALTER HOMOLKA

Let me begin with two assertions: first, that print is different in character from all other media; and, second, that reading is above all a linguistic event; that is to say, the 'content' of written language, wherein its meaning lies, is language. Two less problematic assertions can scarcely be imagined. Of course print is different from other media – each medium is different from every other. And, of course written language consists of language. Of what else could it consist?

Yet these two apparent truisms are quite frequently forgotten, by laymen and 'experts' alike, in the ubiquitous discussion about electronic media and the future of reading. Recent surveys reduce the reading of newspapers, magazines and books to 'media activities' that are both quantifiable and directly comparable with watching television, listening to the radio, going to see films, etc. For decades, scientific inquiry into the psychology of reading has focused on the neurological mechanics of decoding visual symbols, or the minute mechanisms of phoneme recognition – all of which is very interesting, no doubt. But this kind of thinking seems to me to overlook the forest for the trees. Reading and writing are fundamentally a form of linguistic *communication*. A paradigm that conceives of them as merely a system of encoding and decoding, that privileges visual processing over meaning construction, misses the point.

Let me expand on the two above assertions in a way that brings them together. Print – to be understood in this chapter as shorthand for 'typographically-determined visual expression' – is not only different from other media in ways in which the other media are *not* different from each other, but is also deserving of a special category, for reasons explored below. Spoken language is the first and most basic of mankind's many means of communication and meaning construction, and will remain so as long as human beings continue to associate with one another. Written language is different in crucial ways from spoken language. It is none the less rooted in, and intimately related to, the latter. Although writing and especially print in the last few centuries have changed the world and transformed our minds – making possible, among other things, all that we know as modernity – they have done so by virtue of being the medium of *language*, which, it bears repeating, is the fundamental medium through which we explain ourselves and the world to each other and to ourselves.

In this chapter I wish to explore how the printed word, by virtue (paradoxically) of both its dependence on the spoken word and its autonomy, should be seen as something more than a medium. A brief historical survey will give some indication of the extent to which print has transformed and reorganized our world; whilst a look at the work of several modern-day thinkers will suggest how it has transformed our minds. From this perspective, the second part of the chapter will address the issue of publishing and reading in the context of the present-day proliferation of electronic media. I will present some of the empirical evidence about reading trends today, and touch on the vexing issue of literacy, albeit briefly, before closing with some thoughts on what the written word might look like in the coming decades.

Print

'The world changed forever in the mid-fifteenth century, with the invention of movable type.' As with most clichés, there is some truth in this statement, though it is absurdly simplistic as it stands. In fact, the earth did not shake, the heavens did not open, when Gutenberg turned out his first printed pages in Mainz in the early 1450s. Though the techniques of movable-type printing spread quite quickly by the standards of the time, several humble historical facts should be noted. First, the invention was not a singular innovation. Movable type had been employed in China for centuries, and the principles behind Gutenberg's 'invention' were well understood at the time. In fact, it is more helpful to think of 'the printing press' as shorthand for a cluster of developments that came together at this time, including not only the development of metal type, but advances in paper manufacture and the use of oil-based ink. Secondly, it was to take centuries before some of the most important effects of printing manifested themselves. The first books resembled manuscripts almost exactly, and the vast bulk of the first 100 years of printed books continued to be 'medieval'. The Enlightenment and the modern sciences did not spring into existence in print-shops, and books did not suddenly destroy the Church and bring down the old order. Nor is it always easy (or helpful) to try to isolate historical cause and effect, particularly in this case. Even if we grant that the Protestant Reformation of the sixteenth century would not have taken the shape it did without inexpensive printing, can we thus say that printing made it possible? If we acknowledge that the modern sciences as we know them are wholly dependent on the efficient and accurate dissemination of information that printing brought for the first time, are we justified in granting printing a privileged place over numerous other historical factors, political, social, and economic? Was the demand for mass literacy in the nineteenth century (earlier in some places) 'caused' by print?

The difficulty of answering these kinds of questions would suggest extreme caution in attributing significant effects to the medium of print. However, until recently, there was no danger in this regard. Historians of post-Renaissance Europe, and particularly historians of early modern science, generally relegated printing to an extremely minor role, if indeed they mentioned it at all. It was seen as merely a tool, an efficient means of copying. It was only with the pioneering work of Marshall McLuhan in the 1960s, followed by other writers and perhaps most importantly the painstaking research of Elizabeth Eisenstein, that the medium of print was given its due as both a vastly important historical phenomenon, and an extra-historical (that is to say, psychological) organizing force of the first order.[1]

I will have to limit myself to a brief summary of Eisenstein's findings; the interested reader is strongly encouraged to read her work. Eisenstein focuses primarily on the learned professions and sciences. The changes wrought by the printing press on these were deep and far-reaching, and soon spread well beyond the small community of Latin-reading men who at the time constituted the intellectual élite. Not only did printing make it possible for the first time to have diverse texts at one's disposal for comparison and criticism, but it also freed scholars from the time-consuming drudgery of copying. Errors could at last be isolated and eliminated in updated and corrected editions; consensus – requiring as it does common objects of reference – became a possibility; for the first time one could speak of a canon of commonly read works, and growing scholarly collaboration. The precision and exact repeatability of print created a new concern with, and confidence in, the accuracy of maps, mathematical constructions, numbers and figures, diagrams and illustrations, leading directly to advances in all those fields that employed them, and allowing scholars to communicate with each other across linguistic divides, most markedly in the developing 'language of nature', mathematics.

Printing 'was an important precondition for the Protestant Reformation as a whole'; the heart of Luther's project, namely bringing the Bible home (in a quite literal sense), would have been impossible without enormous quantities of printed bibles.[2] Many of the troubles of the Catholic and Protestant churches during the sixteenth century and later, and by extension the sacred/secular divide that became so pronounced in the late Renaissance, are directly attributable to books and mass print. The rise of national languages, and in their wake nationalism, was also underwritten by the medium of print.

What is so special about print? Eisenstein's cautious, carefully documented work emphasizes the empirically visible features of printed works: their accessibility, reproducibility, susceptibility to correction and updating, their fixity and permanence. All of these features are undeniable, and indispensable to understanding Western history from the 1450s to the present. However, there is much more.

Typographic culture

To begin to understand the enormity of typography's influence on the Western mind and Western culture, one must look back two millennia before Gutenberg, to the invention of the phonetic alphabet. Print is, after all, merely the refinement (albeit a profound one) of writing. It is the alphabet – perhaps the most significant innovation in human history – and what it has made possible that underlies any influence that writing or print exerts. The phonetic alphabet for the first time allowed mankind to preserve its language in permanent form, to translate its other senses into sight, to reduce all relations and functions to the visual field. The consequences of this technology are as profound as they are taken for granted by us, who could not conceive of life without literacy. Whereas sound (the dominant, organizing sense in non-literate cultures) is the sense of simultaneity, action, involvement, sight is that of dissection, cool contemplation, distance, *abstraction*. The act of reading isolates the reader, literally and figuratively, and by definition turns her/his attention away from the 'world out there' and towards the world of abstract relations that is written language.

In short, alphabetic writing demands the organization of thought according to the dictates of the sense of sight: clarity, analysis (in the sense of breaking down into parts), detachment, and temporal suspension. It is no accident that the ancient Greeks, who employed the first true phonetic alphabet, originated geometry and logic – even, in the broader sense, extended analytical thought. Using alphabetic writing is itself an analytical exercise; many students of the written word today argue that the very act of writing fosters logical discourse.

After the fall of the Roman empire, which, as Harold Innis points out, could not have existed without paper and writing, a peculiar hybrid, half-oral, half-literate culture (a 'chirographic' or script-based culture) prevailed in Europe until the mid-fifteenth century.[3] For various reasons – socio-cultural but also having to do with the character of script and the physical means of writing – the potential of the phonetic alphabet lay dormant until well after the advent of printing. With typography, however, came the ideal embodiment of the ideals of the alphabet: exactly identical, repeatable atomistic units (letters), and stark abstraction in the visual field, removed from the agency of the human hand. Needless to say, the more mundane aspects of print (foremost the printing press's capacity for mass production), touched on above, account for much of its historical influence. But it is worth considering some less obvious but just as profound effects that can be termed psychological rather than historical.

The contrast between chirographic and typographic forms: the commonplace and the index

The commonplace was (as its name suggests) a ubiquitous form in the late Middle Ages and well into the era of printing. It has since vanished. In essence and origin, it was a means of organizing material for orators. Under various topics or 'places', such as 'causes and effects', 'comparable things', 'contraries', etc., a speaker could find a stock of rhetorical material – sayings, witticisms, etc. The genre expanded to include collections of notable extracts from other works, not necessarily geared toward orators, but still organized rhetorically. The commonplace embodied chirographic culture's rootedness in the oral; writing was an adjunct to speech, a means of preservation, an aid to memory.

The index as we know it only came into regular use with typography and the regular pagination that printing made possible. Its principle of organization is markedly abstract; it is dictated neither by the needs of the reader, nor by the content of the book, but by the arbitrary order of the alphabet. In presenting neat rows of words and page numbers, it dramatizes the striking disengagement of printed words from discourse, their status as spatialized objects, in ways that script never did. The index, moreover, is an exercise in textual analysis that, in conjunction with other practices dictated by the process of printing, led directly to new and rational organizations of knowledge. What makes one word, or one occurrence of a word, more important than another? When does it indicate a significant idea, and when is it passing or incidental? It can readily be seen that this kind of sustained questioning will lead to the kind of close scrutiny and analysis that manuscripts did not support. The index, with its radically abstract, visually-determined character and analytical power is a typographic form *par excellence*.

Isolation and individuality

Sound unites; sight isolates. Sounds come from all directions and demand attention and action, situating the hearer in simultaneity. Visual stimuli invite the separation of seer and seen, subject and object. The sense of sight can parse, divide, free itself from temporality and the need for action. Alphabetic writing demands that all relations be reduced to the visual and abstract (squiggles on a two-dimensional plane), thereby inserting even more separation between the subject (the reader) and the object (the 'referent' of the written word). With silent reading – it is important to note that until printing 'reading' denoted 'reading aloud' – the individual came to be alone in a new way:

... more intensely with print, the individual first becomes aware of himself as capable of thinking for himself to a degree impossible for relatively over-communalized tribal man. Without literacy man tends to solve problems in terms of what people say or do – in the tradition of the tribe, without much personal analysis ... With literacy, the individual finds it possible to think through a situation more from within his own mind out of his own personal resources and in terms of an objectively analyzed situation which confronts him. He becomes more original and individual, detribalized.[4]

It is no accident that the rise of the individual in European culture coincided with the growing dominance of print.

History and progress

One of the widely acknowledged distinctions between medieval and modern man is the latter's ability to view the past from a fixed distance. Practically speaking, to do so was impossible until proper dates could be assigned, tangled chronologies could be unravelled, and better systems for organizing material could be developed. The past had to be organized. And it is only from the perspective of a fixed, orderly history that the concept of progress comes into being. In the most practical and demonstrable way, printing made this possible. But I would also like to suggest that such a 'perspective' ('vantage', 'view point' – all visual terms) is unthinkable without the kind of orderly, linear thought inspired by alphabetic writing, which finds its ideal form in print. Our conception of the past and future is strikingly spatial. We think in terms of time-lines, events distributed over a stretch of time, the future 'stretching out' before us, often in the form of a path or road.

Mass production and applied knowledge

Mass production, and the application of scientific principles to practical tasks, are perhaps the most obvious features of modernity. It is not a commonly appreciated fact, but it is a fact nonetheless, that the first assembly line in human history, 'the first mechanical arrangement to produce complex products made up of replaceable parts, each single product and part exactly like every other', was the printing press.[5] Ong's point in the passage from which this quotation is taken is that mass production first came into being to deal with the needs of the mind, rather than physical needs. It is after all only when man can break up his experience into uniform units that he can then turn this process to his advantage in manufacturing objects. What is it, though, that allows this breaking up of experience in the first place? It is the alphabet. The written alphabet renders speech into a visual code. It is merely one more step to render another complex of relations into explicit visual terms (the key to applied knowledge), and then another, and another. As the alphabet embodies the visualization, lineal organization, and breaking into homogeneous units that are the principles of mass production, it is hardly surprising that their first expression in material terms came about in the effort to materialize and regularize alphabetic writing.

These, then, are some of the ways in which typography, as the ideal medium of alphabetic writing, has shaped our world and the way we think and live. It can be said that the age of typography reached its zenith in Europe and North America from the mid- to late nineteenth century, when mass literacy first became a reality, when newspapers were the only source of news and information for the average citizen, and before the communications revolution of our own century once again altered the way we see the world and ourselves.

Publishing and reading in the late twentieth century

We are living in what has been variously termed a post-industrial, electronic, digital, or information society. Over twenty years ago, Daniel Bell noted that, for the first time in history, over half of the US labour force consisted of information workers.[6] An entire generation has since grown up with computers, world-wide satellite communications, digital recording technology, video machines, and cable television. The pace of change has, if anything, steadily accelerated. Ten years ago, personal computers were relatively primitive and just starting to be popular. Now they are all but ubiquitous, several orders of magnitude faster and more powerful, and cheaper. A CD-Rom disk weighing less than an ounce can contain the text of the entire *Encyclopædia Britannica*; the newest fibre-optic cable will be capable of transmitting the same volume of information from place to place in a single second. By the beginning of the new millennium telecommunications will have overtaken the automotive industry as the most important industrial branch in Western industrialized countries. The projected growth rate for this sector, estimated at between 5 and 10 per cent, exceeds that for the economy overall. I could go on and on, but there is no need. When elected officials start talking about the 'information superhighway', and governments commit massive funds to digital infrastructure, no one can doubt that a transformation has occurred. The task is now to understand what it means – in this case, particularly, what it means for the printed word and reading.

There is no question that the printed media (I refer to newspapers and books; magazines are a different story) have in our century suffered in competition with the electronic media. The newspaper industry in particular has been hard hit, and been forced to change in order to survive. Radio and then television have shown that they can deliver news faster and in a more entertaining and popular format. Both contributed directly to a drastic fall in newspaper readership. Before the penetration of the radio, television, VCR, and stereo into nearly every home in Western industrialized countries, books counted among the most popular forms of home entertainment. This is no longer the case.

Clearly, the electronic media were and are better suited to carry out some of the tasks that print had borne alone – by default, there having been no alternative – for more than four centuries. Listening to a speech on the radio is a closer approximation to being there than reading the text in tomorrow's newspaper. Newsreel footage is often worth a thousand (printed) words. Television is notoriously more seductive in its appeal as an entertainment form than books can ever hope to be. However, the net result of the proliferation of electronic media has been not to render typography obsolete, but to force those industries associated with it to focus on its strengths. Almost fifty years after the introduction of television (in the United States) the daily newspaper is still thriving. Why? Because it has emphasized its advantages over television: portability (one can read it anywhere) and convenience (one can read at one's own speed at any time); in-depth news coverage as well as a broad range of local news and information, neither of which television can support; the provision of reams of information such as tide tables, stock market quotations, and sports statistics; and more 'lifestyle' material – special supplements aimed at businessmen, housewives, automobile enthusiasts, etc.

Though 'general' magazines such as *Life* suffered (and those that survived, such as *Time*, have by and large done so by resembling television more and more), the secret of success in periodical publishing was soon discovered: tailor the material to a specific group, or even one specific need of a specific group, and target that group relentlessly. The remarkable success story of magazines in recent years is well-known. Both newspapers and magazines have tailored themselves to the multiplication of roles and identities, the fragmentation of professions, occupations and interests that characterize our century. It may be added that cable television, with its specialized, specifically targeted channels, is attempting with success to do the same. However, it will never be as successful as books, magazines and newspapers, in that order, in satisfying the particular needs of particular consumers.

As for books: the abject failure of television or radio to serve as a vehicle for serious thought has highlighted the role of the book as bearer of culture, vehicle of reasoned dissent and criticism, medium of knowledge and learning. The book industry has had to scramble to adapt to the ever-changing socio-economic facts of this century as much as, or more than, most. But, except in terms of leisure-time consumption, books and the non-print media cannot generally be said to be in competition, as they are so vastly different. (I am leaving aside for now consideration of computers and digital information delivery.) Before going into these differences and their implications, however, let us look at recent trends in book buying and reading considered as one of many leisure-time activities.

Surveys and statistics

The nature of surveys often precludes the kind of knowledge that we would most like to have. For instance, surveys are incapable of informing us what exactly a reader derives from the books that he/she reads (or the quality of the books), what kind of television programmes a particular viewer watches and what he/she gets out of them, how much of her/his understanding of the world comes from which source, etc. This kind of knowledge is available only anecdotally, if at all. In order to discern larger demographic trends, however, we are obliged to use the blunt tools of social science. This is not to say that the information gathered thereby is useless: far from it. A thoughtful survey can tell us a great deal. Furthermore, the fact that all the major players (economic and political) in our market society base their most important decisions on such information makes it significant, *ipso facto*. My point is that one must recognize the limitations inherent in this kind of data-collection, and form conclusions in a provisional manner.

Provisionally, then, let us look at some recent studies. The 1993 *Consumer Research Study on Book Purchasing*, a 'study revealing the nature of book-buying habits of the American public', ' . . . presents a picture of an industry that is alive and well. Despite concern on the part of many people about the competition posed by other media, people continue to buy more books each year' (pp. 1–3). The study's 12,000 respondents represented a cross-section of American society, and were divided for the purpose of analysis according to age, income, education, and occupation. Regional differences were noted, and results broken down according to outlet type (bookstore, book club, etc.), subject (fiction, travel, etc.), and book type (hardback, mass-market paperback, etc.). Between 1992 and 1993, for example, unit sales of 'technical/science/education' books increased by 18.6 per cent; 'art/literature/poetry' increased by 15.7 per cent; and popular fiction by 9 per cent. Sales of reference books showed the only decline (–1.7 per cent). As could be expected, the most active buyers of books were those with relatively high incomes and high levels of education. On a darker note, roughly half of the participants did not buy a book during the year. Here, of course, we cannot know whether this means that they didn't read (by borrowing, or using a library); nor, conversely, can we tell whether book buyers actually read their books. Still, acknowledging these grey areas, we can still say that, according to this study, book-buying in the United States shows no sign of decline.

Another study presents an even more optimistic picture. An American investment bank estimates that in 1996 the growth rate expected for books (and other specialist information) will be second only to that for cable television and video, and ahead of traditional television, films, newspapers, magazines, audio media and radio.

A 1994 survey conducted in Europe by Bertelsmann presents different information. According to this study, the percentage of 'readers' (defined as reading at least one book a year) in the Netherlands, the UK and Germany is in the 70–80 per cent range, slightly less in France, and in the 50 per cent range in Italy and Spain. Except for the UK, most readers are found in the younger age-groups.

Although the most used medium in leisure-time is television (for instance, an average of 183 minutes per working day in the UK), the survey claims a remarkable average book-reading time (for 'readers'): on average, except in Germany, over one hour per working day. The percentage of 'daily book readers' is similarly heartening (with the exception of Germany, at 18 per cent), ranging from 29 per cent in Italy to 49 per cent in France. The study also found the expected connection between education, upbringing and reading. Though it did not chart trends, being a one-time survey, it did note that the percentage of so-called 'heavy buyers' (those buying more than ten books a year) increased between 1990 and 1994.

Another study, conducted by the 'Reading Foundation' (*Stiftung Lesen*) in Germany in 1992–93, found something regarding television viewing that I will revisit below: the more someone reads, the less that person watches television, statistically speaking. And, further-more, it revealed that the proportion of people who select their television programmes specifically is significantly higher among heavy readers.

Literacy

Much or most of the debate on reading and print is cast in terms of 'literacy'. To say that this term is problematic would be an under-statement; there are as many definitions of 'literacy' as there are writers who employ the term. Should it denote merely the ability to inscribe and sound out words (a better term for which is Seymour Papert's 'letteracy')? Or should it be defined as 'functional literacy': the minimum facility needed to fill out forms, read instructions, and understand official letters, bills, etc.? More alternatives: literacy is the ability to express and understand in writing anything that one could utter or hear in one's spoken language. Or: literacy has more to do with familiarity and grounding in the 'literature' of one's culture ('cultural literacy', which includes, for instance, music and art as well as writing). In this sense, anyone who has not read any of the 'canonical' works of her/his culture cannot be said to be literate.

According to the definition one adopts – if one indeed manages to formulate a useful definition at all – the importance of literacy and its current status vary widely. What almost everyone agrees upon is that: (1) reading and writing are the basis of meaningful participation in society; (2) illiteracy is deplorable and rampant; and (3) something should be done about it.

It is difficult to disagree with any of these statements. An appalling percentage of our populations cannot understand relatively short text passages. According to one study, the figure in Germany alone is 3 million adults; in the United States, 30 million. World-wide, more than 1 billion people cannot make any sense of written words and are unable to write. Speculation on the causes of this crisis, as it is rightly called, is beyond the scope of this essay, as are prescriptions for its amelioration. I must limit myself here to considering why literacy, however one defines it, is important.

First and foremost, literacy is important because the Western world has been based on the printed word for over five centuries. Granted that our century has seen new modes of communication appear, some of which (mainly television) have appeared to dominate certain spheres of human activity, and all of which have affected our way of perceiving the world and relating to others. However, five centuries of history cannot be erased in five decades. Overwhelmingly, our society still organizes itself in terms of written communication. On the most prosaic level, literacy is required to get things done, from paying a telephone bill, to getting a driver's licence, to functioning in the workplace, to seeing what is on television that night. Furthermore, the principles according to which a bureaucracy operates, or a business is run, or domestic policy is shaped, or an automobile works or does not are all tied inextricably to the medium of print (as I hope to have shown above), and only fully explicable therein.

Second, and more importantly, reading and writing are our chief mode of knowledge and understanding – as I touched on above, our very conception of understanding is to a large extent typographically (visually) determined. So not only is an illiterate adult excluded in real ways from society; he or she is also deprived of the language of critical thought. One's choices in this world are clearly delimited by one's ability to sift through the media messages that bombard us day and night, to distinguish fact from assertion, to detach oneself from events – in short, to think critically. In practice, the ability to think critically is contingent upon the ability to read and write.

Television versus reading

Ten years ago, Neil Postman made a compelling case that the language of television was becoming the organizing discourse of American public life.[7] Examples from all areas of American culture were not difficult to find; at the time, after all, a former movie-actor was in the White House. The intervening decade has, if anything, seen his case strengthened. Whatever substance and reasoned debate had once characterized American politics has indisputably disappeared in favour of media image and the sound-bite. As I write, the biggest news story of the decade is the (fully televised) murder trial of a former football star turned corporate spokesman/movie actor, which resembles nothing so much as an especially lengthy and tedious American 'soap opera'. To the extent that Postman's analysis is correct (and it can apply more and more to the situation in Europe), the language of television has shaped public discourse and private life at the expense of the organizing discourse of typography, which had been dominant for centuries. I doubt whether anyone who is taking the trouble to read this book will fail to be alarmed and dismayed at this trend, which Postman characterized as the triumph of entertainment. But before we succumb to gloom, let us take a look at what is meant by the 'language of television'.

Since McLuhan it has been accepted as an axiom that no technology, no medium, is without its particular bias. The biases of print were touched on earlier. The bias of television has first of all to do with its character as presenter of images. The photographic image can only be recognized; by itself it cannot tell us anything. It cannot present an idea or thought, except in so far as we translate it into language. In other words, a photographic image 'cannot deal with the unseen, the remote, the internal, the abstract'.[8] Hence any medium based on the image will also suffer from this deficiency. The rest of television's attributes (as a technological object and as an industry) render it unsuitable for certain ideas and types of discourse – namely those that cannot be reduced to entertainment, those that require a context, those that require more than a few minutes of thought or critical disengagement – those ideas that cannot be seen. The language of television is 'imagery, narrative, presentness, simultaneity, intimacy, immediate gratification, and quick emotional response'.[9] Certainly it is horrible to contemplate the spectre of a society organized along these lines, a culture in which 'television has made entertainment itself the natural format for the representation of all experience'.[10] But we must not overlook the fact that the 'language' of television can never and will never supplant language proper. We still think in words and sentences, and will continue to do so as long as we retain the ability to speak.

In other words, we are primarily linguistic beings: and language will continue to be the primary means by which we constitute and orient ourselves. It is in our nature to make interconnections, to attempt to situate ourselves in a context. Television is by nature a decontextualizing force. There is no connection between a 30-second news story on Middle Eastern terrorism and the 30-second advertisement for chewing gum that follows it – nor is the viewer expected to make connections, or in fact 'do' anything. Television is entertainment. But the serious business of society – feeding, housing, employing the people, conducting science, interacting with other cultures, even manufacturing and marketing (objects as well as 'entertainment products') – is simply not reducible to the entertaining medium of television. However threatening television is to the moral fabric of society, the character of its public discourse, or even our collective attention span, there is no danger of college textbooks being replaced by videos. The one is conducive to thought and understanding, which make possible productive action, the other is not.

In this time of wildly proliferating electronic media, it is more important than ever to be able to situate oneself, to be able to sift critically through the media messages that clamour for our attention every day. Here reading is the key. It has been shown that it is habitual readers who derive the greatest benefit from the vast range of opportunities offered by the media. All manner of studies in Europe and the United States conclude that reading skills are essential for media competence.[11] According to a survey by the Bertelsmann Foundation for the Encouragement of Reading, children who spend the most time reading make the greatest use of media altogether.[12] They are more intensely involved with the medium, whatever its form. To return to a point I made at the beginning of this essay: print – written language – is more than just another medium. Both by virtue of its close relation to speech and its abstraction therefrom, it is the language of thought and understanding.

The future of print

... the media in their succession do not cancel out one another but build on one another. When man began to write, he did not cease talking. Very likely, he talked more than ever; the most literate persons are often enough extraordinarily fluent oral verbalizers as well, although they speak somewhat differently from the way purely oral man does or did. When print was developed, man did not stop writing. Quite the contrary: only with print did it become imperative that everybody learn to write – universal literacy, knowledge of reading and writing, has never been the objective of manuscript cultures but only of print cultures. Now that we have electronic communication, we shall not cease to write and print. Technological society in the electronic stage cannot exist without vast quantities of writing and print.[13]

What are the implications of the present 'digital information revolution' for print and reading? First, let me clarify what I mean by digital information revolution. Advances in computer technology have in recent years made feasible the storage, retrieval and manipulation of vast quantities of information that a few decades ago had to be stored on paper. New communication technologies have made it possible for anyone with a cheap micro-computer and a modem to have access to a good deal of this information. The scientific community was the first group to change their ways of doing things using these technologies – the Internet is in fact the direct descendant of the network established by research institutions in the United States for the purposes of communication and sharing of data. For well over a decade, scientists all over the globe have been communicating with each other electronically, sharing research and even 'publishing' journals without recourse to paper, printers or post. The phenomenon has long since spread to other academic communities, all kinds of organizations, and now private individuals. Though we are far from the constantly hyped ideal of 'all information in all places at all times' – which in my opinion will always remain an ideal – we are indisputably moving in that direction.

Though the computer threatens to provide a more powerful organizing discourse than the television (insofar as it can *incorporate* written language as well as that of television), it is too early to discern clearly the impact of this 'information revolution'. Some implications for the publishing industry are, however, clear. First and foremost, all manner of reference works, from statistical tables to dictionaries to encyclopaedia, and particularly scientific publications, are now being delivered via CD-Rom and other digital means, and the trend will, if anything, intensify. The computer is clearly superior to print in its capacity to let the 'reader' search for, access and manipulate information. And the benefits of being able to incorporate sounds and moving images in text are profound, as are the associated possibilities of hypertext. It remains to be seen how the general populace will take to 'interactive fiction' (in which the reader can influence the direction of the plot) and the delivery of traditional literature, fiction and non-fiction, by digital means. For now, formidable obstacles remain – principally the limitations of the computer screen. However, it would be naïve to assume that these obstacles will remain for long.

It would be naïve, in fact, to do more than speculate in the most general manner in this regard. The development of technologies and their effects are quite simply unpredictable. I therefore intend to limit myself in this section to making a few general points.

Information as a linguistic event

As Mark Poster trenchantly observes in his *The Mode of Information*, information is not merely a commodity, as has been postulated by writers on 'post-industrial society' since Daniel Bell in the early 1970s.[14] Hence it is dangerous to base social or economic theorizing on that premise. Much as information is *treated* as a commodity by entertainment and information industries, that is, is marketed and sold, it is important to differentiate packages of information from traditional consumer products. For one thing, once purchased, most information (I include here recorded music, broadcast television, and computer programs, as well as traditional 'print-encoded' information) can be replicated perfectly and cheaply. One cannot say this of traditional products such as shoes or cameras – or even, for that matter, of books, as it is still generally cheaper and easier to buy a book than to replicate it. Further, information is 'consumed' in an entirely different way; when one is 'through' with it, if that can be said to happen, the product still remains. For these reasons we can say that information does not obey the traditional rules of material goods. In the case of print-encoded information, there is a further crucial difference: namely, that receiving it is a linguistic event, with all that that implies. Treating communications as an economic rather than as a linguistic fact obscures both the new possibilities for disseminating information opened up by the new technologies and the way these technologies affect the way we communicate.[15]

Information versus knowledge

Information in and of itself is useless. What the cybernetic visionaries whose mantra is 'all information in all places at all times' neglect to consider is that few people actually want more information. We are inundated with information. What is desperately needed are ways to organize it all. Information does not set us free; knowledge does. Books have been the traditional vessels of knowledge for most of recorded history and, in the absence of competition from electronic media, are still the prime medium of knowledge and wisdom today. It is my belief that, whatever form they take, books (relatively lengthy, self-contained, text-based exposition) will continue in this role.

The typographic word

What is also traditionally ignored by those who prophesy the death of print and books is that most information, digitally stored or otherwise, is in the form of print. Whether one reads a journal article on paper or on a computer screen, one is still reading. I am prepared to contemplate a world many years hence in which actual paper books are a rarity; but I cannot imagine the disappearance of print-based written language. This is not to say that language will not change, perhaps even fundamentally, over a period of years – though here we have entered the realm of absolute speculation. Language certainly changed as the result of alphabetic writing, and later of print, so why shouldn't electronic communication have its effect as well? Electronic mail, with its half oral/half epistolary protocols, possibilities for playing with identities, obscuring gender, destabilizing existing hierarchies, etc., is one medium to watch. Recently writers have pointed to the 'smiley' language invented by Internet users, which is based on hundreds of variations on the sideways smiling face – :) – which convey, generally, the feelings of those who deploy them. In essence, however, what we are confronting here is what literate Europeans faced in the fifteenth century: a new means of encoding written language. I will grant that the modifications of text offered by computers (e.g. hypertext, 'iconography', the supplements of sound and moving images) are more dramatic than those offered by the printing press. Furthermore, I realize that, by virtue of its organizing principles, the computer can be said to have its own logic and language. None the less, it is not and will never be our language, as we are not machines and do not work like them. And, whatever form written language takes, it will still be written language – perhaps not as linearly oriented as traditional print, perhaps accompanied by sounds and images, but written language all the same, with its grammar, syntax, abstractness, and great explanatory and organizing power.

Final thoughts

Horst Opaschowski, from the BAT Leisure Research Institute in Hamburg, recently claimed that 'if the present dramatic rise in the number of non-readers and those who do not buy books continues, the year 2000 will see two thirds of German citizens never holding a book in their hands'. Given what we know of the trends, this claim seems excessive. Nonetheless, despite the current health of the book-publishing industry and the encouraging results of the studies cited in this chapter, there is cause for grave concern. Studies have shown that the gateway to reading is narrative fiction, and it is precisely this genre that has shown the most dramatic decline in recent years. This, I believe, is directly traceable to competition from television and computer games. More importantly, the habits of reading are traditionally formed at a young age. But it is clear that the electronic media, particularly television, have the effect of reducing children's attention span and capacity for sustained engagement of the kind required by reading.

Reading does need to be encouraged. It is by no means threatened with extinction by either technological or social forces, but it is nonetheless unarguable that our children are reading less and less as more and more entertainment becomes available. Fewer men and women are emerging from educational institutions with the literacy skills needed in today's workplace. The economic consequences of illiteracy are widely known and much lamented. But to view literacy purely from the economic standpoint can be harmful. No one learns to read just so that he/she can interpret technical manuals and write acceptable business letters. The key to fostering literacy is to show (hopefully young) readers the pleasures of reading, the worlds that it opens up to the imagination and understanding. Whatever else educators and writers on the subject disagree about, there is a consensus that reading is both essential to functioning in our society and a crucial ingredient in personal enrichment and growth. Most of the values held dear by our cultures – democracy, universal education, freedom of expression, individual rights – would not have developed, and cannot be sustained, without a literate citizenry.

What can be done? Rather than mouthing the usual platitudes about schooling, eradication of poverty as a precondition, instilling in parents the danger of television and the importance of teaching their children to read – all of which are quite important – I would like to suggest that the publishing industry itself has an invaluable opportunity. The fragmentation of media markets, in the United States and especially in Europe with its many cultures and languages, is a reality. Consumers are demanding products, entertainment, and information tailored to their specific needs and desires. The traditional mass media are adapting as quickly as they can (the proliferation of cable television being one prominent example), but books enjoy a unique advantage over the traditional electronic media in this regard. The fact that in 1992 roughly 844,000 book titles were published world-wide, as against roughly 10,000 films being produced, should give us a clue that the key is in diversity, local products for specific tastes and needs. Books (and magazines) will remain uniquely suited to satisfying the needs of individuals as opposed to faceless 'consumers'.

Book publishers should embrace the new digital technologies, release products on CD-Rom and whatever other forms become available, combine text with sounds and moving images, experiment with hypertext and interactive fiction, and above all do whatever they can to make books and reading available and desirable to everyone. It is in their own interest – and in the interests of a competitive economy, a functioning democracy and all the ideals that it embodies, and the personal development of every citizen.

References

1. M. McLuhan, *The Gutenberg Galaxy: The Making of Typographic Man*, Toronto: Toronto University Press, 1962; W. Ong, *The Presence of the Word: Some Prolegomena for Cultural and Religious History*, New Haven, CT: Yale University Press, 1967; W. Ong, 'Reading,

technology and the nature of man: an interpretation', *Yearbook of English Studies* 10, London: Modern Humanities Research Association, 1980, pp. 132–49; J. Goody, *Literacy in Traditional Societies*, Cambridge: Cambridge University Press, 1968; J. Goody, *The Logic of Writing and the Organization of Society*, Cambridge: Cambridge University Press, 1986; E. Havelock, *Preface to Plato*, Oxford: Basil Blackwell, 1963; E. Havelock, *The Literate Revolution in Greece and its Cultural Consequences*, Princeton, NJ: Princeton University Press, 1982; W. Frawley, *Text and Epistemology*, Norwood, NJ: Ablex, 1987; N. Postman, *Amusing Ourselves to Death*, London: Methuen, 1985; N. Postman, *Technopoly: The Surrender of Culture to Technology*, New York: Knopf, 1992; E. Eisenstein, *The Printing Press as an Agent of Change*, Cambridge: Cambridge University Press, 1979.

2. E. Eisenstein, *The Printing Press in Early Modern Europe*, Cambridge: Cambridge University Press, 1983, p. 151.

3. H. Innis, *The Bias of Communications*, Toronto: Toronto University Press, 1951.

4. Ong, *The Presence of the Word*, p. 134.

5. Ong, 'Reading, technology and the nature of man', p. 141.

6. D. Bell, *The Coming of Postindustrial Society*, New York: Basic Books, 1973.

7. Postman, *Amusing Ourselves to Death*.

8. Postman, *Amusing Ourselves to Death*, p. 73.

9. Postman, *Technopoly*, p. 16.

10. Postman, *Amusing Ourselves to Death*, p. 89.

11. Bundesminister für Bildung und Wissenschaft (ed.), *In Sachen Lesekultur*, Bonn, 1991; Verlag Bertelsmann Stiftung, *Medienkompetenz als Herausforderung an Schule und Bildung. Ein deutsch-amerikanischer Dialog*, Gütersloh: Bertelsmann, 1992.

12. Bertelsmann, *Medienkompetenz als Herausforderung*.

13. Ong, *The Presence of the Word*, pp. 88–9.

14. M. Poster, *The Mode of Information*, Oxford: Polity Press/Basil Blackwell, 1990.

15. Poster, *The Mode of Information*, p. 28.

8

On Being Passionate about Standards: Promoting the Voice of Aesthetics in Broadcasting and Multimedia

KENNETH DYSON

A television programme is not a commodity. It might become one, but it begins as a labour of love. To make money in television you must first make things, and the things you make are things of the spirit.
Clive James, speech to the Royal Television Society, May 1991

During the twentieth century the philosophical foundations of the debate about culture have shifted from the question 'what is the essence of culture and its real definition?' (the question that preoccupied Matthew Arnold, as we saw in the introduction) to the question 'how is the term culture used?'. This process of abandoning the so-called 'essentialist fallacy', according to which all cultural works share an essential quality, has created an impression of culture as an elusive thing. In one interpretation it is an open-textured empirical term, whose only essence is its incompleteness and permanent possibility of vagueness.[1] Thus culture embraces 'anything that is meaningful'; or 'any set of symbols organized by way of language or in some other meaningful pattern'; or is even just 'context', a matter of the way in which we continually reconstruct our lives.[2] Defined in these sociological terms, it involves genres of 'popular culture' (like the music video or the television quiz show or soap opera) as well as 'works of art' such as the television drama. In another interpretation, culture is simply an emotively charged word that is used to convey approval of certain qualities (say of form, feeling or expressiveness) of particular works; or has just a 'performative' meaning as a linguistic act of commendation.[3] Thus the 'culture' of British television drama productions like *Brideshead Revisited* or *The Singing Detective* is contrasted with the 'trivia' of such television quiz shows as *Sale of the Century* or soap operas like *Dallas*. Here the aesthetic dimension of the concept is being identified, but with the stress on the linguistic acts – emotivism and commendatory meanings – attached to it.

These developments in interpretation have profoundly discredited past efforts at 'essentialist' definitions of culture. At the same time – as we saw in Chapter 1 – they have introduced powerful currents of subjectivism and relativism into cultural studies, represented in particular since the 1970s by post-structuralist analysis of media discourse in its various forms. Culture is then prey to the implications of the belief in the inherent emptiness of words; its meaning derived from its context, above all its economic and political context.[4] From this foundation it is possible to point to the myth of culture and its insubstantiality, as illustrated by the way in which its standards are ignored, inconsistently applied and manipulated. The debate about cultural standards and about standards of objectivity and impartiality can be demystified and the ideologies that support them discredited.[5]

The central argument of this chapter is that, though culture is socially and historically constituted, being continuously remade and redefined under the impact of technological, commercial and political pressures, it continues to depend fundamentally on standards. These standards are ethical and aesthetic, to do with the discrimination between good and bad, right and wrong. They have to do with principles of media use and criteria of accurate, objective and balanced reporting (Lübbe's chapter); with public-interest arguments about the rights of the citizen (Hoffmann-Riem's chapter); and with criteria of aesthetic judgement. In this chapter we are concerned to rescue the idea of culture as aesthetic experience, as an activity of discrimination, and to point to culture's 'amazing trick', the trick by which it can rebuild itself under the pressures of the ever-changing world.

But we should not be complacent about this potential for culture to rebuild itself. Part of the problem has been within media studies/ cultural studies itself, represented in the hegemonic projects of structuralism and poststructuralism outlined in the introductory chapter: for neither was equipped or motivated to develop and refine standards. The other part of the problem has been the way in which the clamour of scientific, commercial and associated political voices in the wider public debate about new media and 'multimedia' has drowned out the distinctive voices of aesthetics and ethics. The 'faith in machinery' represented by the economic potential of 'multimedia' as a 'cultural industry' has displaced attention away from an appreciation of the importance of aesthetic perception and judgement to the enrichment of our common life.

As the introductory chapter argued, this appreciation of aesthetic experience must be grounded in a recognition of the distinction between our 'ordinary selves' and our 'best selves', between the freedom to say and do as we like and the freedom to educate our tastes and, in Matthew Arnold's words, to get 'to know, on all the matters which most concern us, the best which has been thought and said in the world'. The novelist E. M. Forster told the story of an old woman who, asked if she was happy and enjoying what she was getting, replied: 'How do I know what I like, till I see what I can have?'

Aesthetic perception and aesthetic judgement

We have noted that culture is an open-ended and contested concept: that it has, for instance, sociological as well as aesthetic meanings. Even in its aesthetic sense contested views abound about what constitutes a 'work of art' and how a work of art is to be interpreted and evaluated. But, before writing off aesthetic judgements as simply endlessly contested, there are two crucial distinctions to be borne in mind: between observation and aesthetic perception; and between mere subjective preference or liking and aesthetic perception.

Aesthetic perception has to do with a special 'ability to *notice* or *discern* things', distinct as a perceptual mode from observation.[6] Just as observation is under certain controls, so aesthetic perception involves certain independent standards in terms of which one looks 'revealingly' at things, prehends aspects that 'animate' them, and enters into a special kind of intimacy with them: the intimacy of contemplative delight. This underlying 'objectivity' of aesthetic experience helps to frame and control aesthetic judgements, however contested they may remain. It makes it possible to educate those judgements. It also enables us to share with each other in an expressive portrayal of feelings and imaginative insights. We are able to do so by recognizing, interpreting and evaluating how 'materials' (words, gestures, pictures, musical notes) have been used in a 'medium', the 'form' in which they are composed and the way in which they reveal 'content' and illuminate 'subject matter' in new ways.

'Materials', 'medium', 'form', 'content' and 'subject matter' constitute the key components of the work of art as an aesthetic object; they provide the aspects that 'animate' it, like values and intensities of screen space, colour, lighting, speaking, gesture, pose or notes. The materials from one side, and the subject matter from the other, both in a sense external, are transfigured in the work of art as aesthetic object – in its medium, form and style, and content.[7] The artist works on the materials at her/his disposal; uses their distinctive qualities to compose a work of art (the medium); seeks to arrange the medium's elements as values in aesthetic space (form), perhaps achieving some recognizable and distinctive pattern (style); and seeks to articulate in its medium and form some meaningful subject matter (the content). By contrast, the objective criteria that control observation are designed for the purpose of a rational understanding of the world as physical objects: as individuals, states, companies, etc. They are motivated by an impulse of inquiry rather than of contemplative delight. Their central purpose is not to animate our experience of the world.

Another fundamental distinction is between feelings of pleasure and aesthetic experience.[8] Pleasure refers to practical activities by means of which one seeks to satisfy one's desires or to avert what one regards as unpleasant or unacceptable: by, say, watching sports on television or playing video games on the computer for the excitement that they offer or escaping from the daily routine into the fantasy world of a television soap opera. Being entertained in these ways is fundamentally different from the activity of 'poetic imagining' that is basic to aesthetic experience. Poetic imagining is a contemplative activity. It is a matter of choosing and arranging images (sounds, visual patterns, speech, gestures, shapes, etc.), considering how they will appear together so as to provide delight.

In Samuel Taylor Coleridge's famous words on poetic imagination in *Biographia Literaria*, ch. 4:

> It dissolves, diffuses, dissipates, in order to re-create . . . it struggles to idealize and to unify. It is essentially *vital*, even as all objects (as objects) are essentially fixed and dead.
>
> [It involves] the union of deep feeling with profound thought: the fine balance of truth in observing, with the imaginative faculty in modifying the objects observed; and above all the original gift of spreading the tone, the *atmosphere* and with it the depth and height of the ideal world around forms, incidents, and situations, of which,

for the common view, custom had bedimmed all the lustre, had dried up the sparkle and the dewdrops.

Clearly, not all activities of assembling and juxtaposing images represent poetic imagination. In helping us to distinguish the poetic imagination from lower-order imaginative activity Coleridge's characterization of 'fancy' is instructive. 'Fancy' juxtaposes images, but it does not fuse them into an expressive unity. It merely constructs patterns out of ready-made images, being reliant on using the results of previous imaginative activity. 'Fancy' is content to amuse and titillate by aggregating such images. 'Poetic imagination' aims to provide meaningful experience, 'to awaken the mind's attention from the lethargy of custom', to vitalize the otherwise fixed and dead objects of our world, by 'hovering' between images and modifying our experience of the world. Coleridge contrasts the activity of clothing scenes and people with our own thoughts and feelings and the activity of *thinking* ourselves into the thoughts and feelings of others in circumstances wholly and strangely different from our own.

In looking at television for purposes of pleasure the appropriate questions to ask are about whether one has been excited (say by an 'action-packed' film or sports event), amused (by a situation comedy) or relaxed (by being transported into a fantasy world by a soap opera or drama series). But the kind of question one asks of aesthetic experience is different; it has to do with the quality of images as revealed by the delight that they afford, by the way in which materials and subject matter are animated and enriched by fresh, vivid, yet precise images, conveyed by rhythm of sound, use of light and shade, visual angle, diction or gesture. Drawing on Coleridge's distinction, television offers enormous scope to indulge the faculty of fancy. But it can also aspire to poetic imagining. The value of Coleridge's distinction is that it points not only to an observable difference between kinds of television and media imagining but also to a profound distinction in our ways of responding to experience.

Though culture in its aesthetic sense remains a normative concept, it presupposes some ideal of independent standards in terms of which it is possible to make an educated critical appreciation of television programmes and other cultural products. Aesthetics is not simply a matter of variable personal tastes or socially constructed meanings, as argued respectively by radical liberalism and structuralism. It is not captured by pointing to television's 'bardic' function of affirming and celebrating a community identity in the manner of the traditional storyteller and poet; or by identifying its political function in providing control by means of an ideological dominance.[9] Culture as aesthetic experience is a matter of aesthetically *educated* perception by means of which it is possible to discriminate between good and bad. It means a particular kind of perceptual sophistication, involving the recognition that there are good reasons for seeing something as a work of art that are based on an appeal to independent criteria. A strong as opposed to a weak aesthetic judgement characterizes its content, form and medium; it takes account of the expressive portrayal of a significant subject matter and the transfiguration of good-quality materials. As one or more of these items is subtracted or minimized, so the status of a cultural product as a work of art comes into question.

Aesthetic perception is a matter of learning to see what is relevant to critical aesthetic judgement. The result may still be differences of interpretation. Some, for instance, will give priority to content values in aesthetic judgement: what is important for them is that a work should be animated internally by a significant social theme or human experience. Hence soap operas with a focus on social drama, like *Brookside* on Britain's Channel Four, are more aesthetically convincing than escapist soap operas; American movies for television like *Holocaust* or *Roots* are deserving of aesthetic status in a way not typical of this genre. For others, aesthetic judgement concentrates around the values of the medium, on how the images are formulated. What is important here is the loving and skilful use of the properties of the medium – of its sound and visual properties in the case of television, of the qualities of the script as material, of acting performance, of camera work, of scenic work, etc. Content is essentially secondary. Though normative talk (even in describing art) is a necessary component of aesthetic judgement, given that it is about delight, and though angled seeing is probably unavoidable, it is possible to identify independent criteria in terms of which to judge that reasons for preferring one work over another are more or less well-grounded.

Aesthetics endows us, then, with a language with which to discuss quality, albeit one that is characteristically normative. When critically appraising television programmes whose achievements cut right across the different aspects of aesthetic experience to fuse together materials, medium, form, content and subject matter into an expressive coherent whole that affords delight, we use terms like 'powerful', 'compelling' and 'moving'. In this way we are recognizing the vitality that comes from the way in which the qualities of these properties have been fused. Each property has in turn its own language for characterizing quality. The content may be 'profound', 'expressive', 'revealing' and 'insightful'; the medium and form can be 'eloquent', 'sensuous', 'audacious', 'delicate', 'rhapsodic', 'witty', 'balanced', 'forceful'.[10] And, of course, the complexity of the criteria on which aesthetic judgement draws leaves room for differentiated evaluations of the achievements in the component aspects. We may for instance condone a lapse in the quality of plot because of the character interest that a programme contains. In this sense aesthetic judgements of television programmes will remain a 'rule-of-thumb' matter. Even so, we do carry a scale of values by which we know that *Brideshead Revisited* is a work of art and other television dramas are not. Such standards have to do with what the contents tell us about the human condition; how the form is managed, for instance in terms of 'rounded' characterization, development of plot and the management of language; and what the experience does to expand the bounds of our imagination and to make us look at the human condition with new interest and even joy.

Television as medium and art form

There are considerable difficulties in applying criteria of aesthetic judgement in the case of television – and probably even more so in the case of the computer-based multimedia. Looked at as a whole, it is far from being a 'pure' art form. It is muddied by, and mixed with, non-aesthetic modes of perception and communication, including as it does news and documentaries, for which the criteria of achievement relate to the accuracy, impartiality and balance with which the world is represented on the screen, and entertainment, which is valued by the feelings of pleasure that it induces and the degree to which desires are satisfied. Poetic imagining is an intermittent rather than continuous, let alone dominant, feature of television's complex, radically heterogeneous activities. It cedes priority to more insistent practical activities which may use aesthetic devices to 'move' the viewer but which manipulate images in an instrumental way, whether to reproduce the world on our screens more vividly or to entertain. The result is a prevalence of 'ordinariness' and literalness: in short, a relative lack of symbolic density in most genres of television.[11]

To complicate matters further from an aesthetic point of view, television has an extraordinary capacity for 'cultural ingestion', as a 'staging' area that draws to itself and incorporates other media: theatre, cinema, newspapers, the pop music industry, education.[12] Routinely it uses the contents of other media as its own raw material, sometimes content to relay that material (the film, the concert, the sport event), most often imposing its own nature as a medium.[13] But, in consequence, television is rarely a pure medium with its own defined artefacts.

Key problems in the aesthetic judgement of television relate to its specific character as a technology combining sound and vision, as offering a multi-channel experience, and as being physically defined as the 'box in the corner'. First, being electronic and visual, it offers opportunities for 'liveness', 'immediacy' and 'dramatic representation' denied to photography and the press, for instance in news reporting.[14] With technological advances in the form of new light-weight cameras and sound recording equipment, and not least satellite technology, the capacity to show 'real' action 'as it happens' has expanded enormously. In addition to its impact across the range of television output, whole new channels have appeared to exploit these new opportunities as 'live' television and 24-hour news. Here lies one of the great attractions of television as a medium: it offers the promise of more direct information and of a more vivid and embracing sensory experience of 'real' events and 'real' people than other media. These characteristics of 'immediacy' and 'liveness' have in turn promoted a freeing of television practices from the dominance of a print-based literary culture in the direction of reasserting the values of an oral culture.[15] In the process it has demoted the values of precision in language, rigour in analysis, originality of the individual author, detachment, objectivity and contemplation. As we shall see below, this cultural shift is most pronounced in entertainment programmes. But, having roots in certain properties of the medium, this shift has spread its effects into other programme areas.

A second technical characteristic of television is the competition between channels for audience attention. With the advent of new cable technologies, satellite broadcasting and digital compression the rapid process of expansion of channels changes the viewing experience. 'Multi-channel' systems offer new pleasures of channel 'grazing', 'surfing' or 'zapping'. With increased channels two changes seem likely to take effect: first, the toleration level for low intensity of action on screen may decrease; and, secondly, the tolerance period may diminish. Faced with a shift from 'whole programme' to 'part programme' viewing, in fact predating digital television, broadcasters have been under pressure to intensify dramatic action and sensationalize contents to capture restless viewers. Implications for the quality of news and current affairs and drama programming are on the whole negative.[16] Barwise and Ehrenberg have noted how, compared to print media, television viewers tend to be less selective and differentiated in their use of the medium.[17] In part this difference reflects the greater effort required for reading (see Homolka's chapter); in part 'channel-switching'.

Thirdly, being concentrated on a small screen, television induces stylistic intimacy in the form of a preponderance of medium-shot and close-up camera work and a tendency to use relatively shallow focus.[18] This reduced visual scale compared to the cinema also throws greater weight on the expressiveness of acting performance and, to a greater extent than in the theatre, on intimately minute facial expression and gesture.[19] On the other hand, the reduced visual intensities of television, compared to cinema, mean that in seeking to realize its potential aesthetic values television drama is more script-based.[20] It offers less scope for visual compositions in depth, for using camera to develop a way of seeing using deep focus, long takes and wide shots in, say, the style of Jean Renoir.

Fourth, being located and watched in the private domestic context of the home, television must counter distraction (the so-called 'regime of the glance' as opposed to the 'concentrated gaze' typical of the cinema). It does so by a reliance on vivid sound and on the intensity and energy of melodrama to attract the viewer's glance. Hence, though television combines visual images and sound, its programming tends to be 'sound-led' (with, for instance, striking title music to re-engage the attention of viewers).[21] It also relies on intense emotional confrontations, with appropriate musical underscoring and use of the zoom lens, as for instance in soap operas like *Dallas* and *Dynasty*. This domestic dimension also encourages a focus around 'friendly', 'warm' personalities – who in close up become more or less life-size on the television screen (unlike the cinema screen) and can engage in 'direct address' to the viewers in a unique manner.[22] Finally, it fosters a media contents that gravitates towards personal stories as narrative material, preferring to domesticate public issues in this way – not just in television drama but also in news, current affairs and documentaries.[23] The establishment of 'intimacy' in both style and content becomes a preoccupation of television as a medium.[24] Again, as we shall see below, these characteristics of the medium have favoured its bias towards popular culture programmes. 'One-off' and serial form television drama and news, current affairs and documentary programmes have shown that the medium is capable of more fully engaging audiences, whether in offering them contemplative delight or as concerned citizens.

In these various ways television technology conditions the production process, the way in which television messages are encoded, what the message becomes and how stories are told. Control of screen space takes on its own distinctive bounded dynamics as directors manipulate camera space (the horizontal field of view – close-up, medium shot issues – and camera proximity and angle to performers) and performer space (line of sight and depth) to reinforce narrative. Lighting too, particularly in the form of light–dark contrast, offers expressive qualities, alongside set design, as a means of articulating space and focusing attention.[25] But, as developments since the 1980s have demonstrated, ongoing technological developments have altered the constraints within which television production operates. Traditionally, television was primarily focused around multi-camera studio production. This production format produced a different narrative structure from that of cinema. It meant a tendency towards a different and longer basic unit, the segment, so that greater continuity in the form of a scene lasting several minutes could be sustained.[26] Film narrative, by contrast, was defined by the mobility and dynamics of the 'single shot'. With the advent of the 'single camera' operation in the 1980s television and cinema converged as media; short filmic takes were in. New lightweight cameras also opened up new opportunities for 'fly-on-the-wall' programmes.

It is tempting to conclude that such characteristics as 'liveness', 'immediacy', 'sociability', melodrama and a shift away from the values of a literary culture towards 'orality' disenfranchise television from the category of aesthetic experience. It appears as a cultural form dedicated to the ephemeral images associated with entertainment and information/representation: as favouring action over the development of character interest and clash of ideas: as compromised in aesthetic terms by its low symbolic density. Seen from the perspective of the criteria of aesthetic judgement outlined here there is real substance in much of this interpretation and evaluation of television. It raises serious aesthetic problems as a medium. Yet such a conclusion does not mean that entertainment and news/current affairs/documentary programmes are valueless. On the contrary, they have their own values, but they are different from those of aesthetic experience. They deserve the label cultural, but they do not exist mainly to provide culture as an aesthetic experience. These cultural genres invite other standards of judgement. Do they fulfil the known expectations of the viewer? Is the movement of the plot sufficient to engage attention? Are climaxes managed well? Do they meet the needs of viewers who after a hard day's work need a means of relaxation and escape? Do they clearly inform the viewer? More positively, television offers an enormously exciting aesthetic challenge. This challenge is offered most directly in the genre of television drama where television has most promise as an art form. The challenge is to bring together the different arts of the scriptwriter, the camera-person, the actor, the composer, musicians, the set designer and the costume designer into a coherent convincing expressive whole. This challenge makes television drama one of the most important sites of artistic work and aesthetic experience in modern society. But the question remains as to whether economic and technological changes sweeping through the media are dissipating the will and capability of media companies, public service as well as private, to take up that challenge.

 ## Television as cultural experience

Though the specifics of television technology create a powerful conditioning framework for its activities as a medium, technology does not define or account for the complex range of programmes and viewing relations that television embraces. It is this radical complexity that makes generalizations about the relations between technology and cultural forms and contents in television so hazardous. Before we define more precisely the cultural problems besetting television in the age of new media, it is important to establish some distinctions with reference to television as medium. They relate to the different kinds of cultural experience offered by television and underline its extraordinary complexity and heterogeneity. To make matters worse, it is far from easy simply to pigeonhole individual programmes into specific genres. Some of the most interesting programmes develop precisely from the way in which they defy established categories. Nevertheless, the broad distinctions offered below retain a heuristic value.

Television as an experience of pleasure

To begin with, there is a huge realm of what is generally called '*popular culture*'. It embraces such cultural products as advertisements, music videos, video games, variety shows, children's cartoons, quiz shows, talk shows, situation comedies, soap operas, 'made-for-television' movies and sport. The various genres of popular culture specialize in offering the pleasures of entertainment, providing a mixture of relaxation, escapist 'fairy stories' and excitement. Their subject matter and content is not demanding; they gravitate in content to the 'sensational' and in performance to the 'intense', 'vivid' and 'energetic', aiming to retain the viewer's attention and typically responding to the discipline imposed by frequent commercial breaks (as in the narrative structure of the soap opera); they tend to succumb to the embrace of the 'personal interest' story or to being 'host'- or 'presenter'-centred (as in, respectively, the made-for-television movie and the talk show); and they approximate more closely to the model of culture as a (partly standardized) industrial system of mass production and distribution, being on the whole relatively inexpensive and quick to produce.[27] In the process the particular characteristics of television as a medium are being exploited: the intimacy and realism induced by the small screen (as opposed to theatre), and the family context of viewing deriving from its domestic location in the home (unlike cinema).[28]

But, above all, the popularity of these genres derives from public demand for entertainment. People want to escape from the constraints and boredom of everyday life; they need to relax from domestic and job-related stress; and they enjoy being excited.[29] It is the combination of this scope to capture and retain a 'mass' audience (and hence attract advertising income or legitimate the licence fee) with the competitiveness of 'ratings wars' that pushes popular culture programme making towards a 'formula-based' approach, thereby driving out aesthetic values. The 'formula-based' approach involves beginning with a slot in the schedule, deciding how big a rating you want from that slot, and constructing programmes accordingly by reference to the established success of particular genres (say crime series) and actors. Drama ceases to be script-driven; the writer is expected to be part of a team-based production process in which authority shifts from the author to the market-responsive scheduler and commissioning editor. The result is typically 'flat', 'two-dimensional' characterization, built around 'a single idea or quality' and without much individualizing detail or complexity of psychological motivation; dialogue short of fresh and vivid imagery and forceful lively diction; and plots that are predictable and lack development.[30]

In the interpretation of Fiske and Hartley, drawing on Ong's seminal work, television's textual forms take on the qualities of an oral rather than literary culture. They incorporate and use the simple, formulaic and repetitive forms of gossip and direct personal address, along with close reference to lived experience, so that they become a part of shared family life and chatter at work. By drawing on these attributes of oral culture television seeks to provide audience pleasure in the form of feelings of intimacy and identification with familiar characters and situations: for instance, in soap operas and talk shows.[31] In this way television can achieve the extraordinary balancing act of combining ephemeral images with audiences whose sensory attention is absorbed. A key buzzword for this type of programming is 'bonding' with the channel: identified by Rupert Murdoch as the goal of his Fox Broadcasting in the United States and serving as a background idea behind the BBC's *People and Programmes* document of February 1995. But there are costs in this pursuit of oral culture: in a lessening of respect for precision of language, for rigour of analysis, for the originality of the individual author, for detachment and for contemplation.

This market-driven process does not mean that production values are kept uniformly and consistently low. Audiences can become bored and switch off or over, looking for something different. Viewers become experienced and competent in using and evaluating these genres, and in those terms are able to make their own judgements of quality based on the values associated with these genres. This factor of viewer competence, combined with the opportunistic motive of competing for audience attention, is a force for product improvement: for increasing the symbolic density of television advertising and using more non-stereotypical representations; for the better researched, glossy entertainment show; or for the superior characterization and acting performances of crime stories like *Prime Suspect* and *Cracker* from Britain's Granada Television or *Inspector Morse* from Central Television. Advertisers may also be more attracted by the kind of viewer to whom they gain access ('quality demographics') than by the size of audience.[32] American programmes like *Northern Exposure*, *Hill Street Blues* and *Cheers* and British programmes like *Yes, (Prime) Minister* and *Fawlty Towers* offered instances of how the constraints of 'formula' comedy and drama could be overcome.

Despite these countervailing pressures in the direction of respect for aesthetic values creative writers and actors are, on the whole, not attracted or given an outlet for serious artistic development in these genres. And the more these genres dominate scheduling, and their values and practices cross-fertilize news and current affairs and television drama in general, the greater the threat to the ethical and aesthetic qualities of television as a medium. It may be possible to speak of popular culture as offering some kind of aesthetic experience (say the quality of acting in a soap opera or situation comedy, even the iconography of an advertisement).[33] But limitations of subject matter in genres oriented to provide pleasure, the logistical demands of production schedules, and their combined effects on production values, preclude that experience being linked in a general way to any serious notion of television programmes as works of art.

Television as an activity of inquiry and instruction

In addition to the pleasures of entertainment, television offers another kind of experience – *inquiry* and *instruction* – in the form of news and current affairs programmes, documentaries and specialized programming about the arts (book and food programmes, for instance), travel, wildlife and science. Television's mission to inform, educate and explain is typically identified as central to its cultural mission, involving high-status genres essentially concerned (unlike entertainment) with the public sphere. It has also been seen as the special function and legitimation of public service broadcasting, conferring authority on programming and acting as a 'flagship'. The educational role can involve specially designed courses, leading for instance to a university degree (the Open University in Britain being a model here). Here again computer and cable technologies offer new prospects for interactive learning in the 'multimedia' age, as well as customized information services that can be actively interrogated by the user. In providing these types of programme television is dealing in sensory evidence: relaying events, providing commentary and undertaking investigation.

Information and educational programming is about culture and quality in the ethical sense, raising issues about whether the citizen is being properly informed and whether opportunities are being equalized (points pursued in the chapters by Lübbe and Hoffmann-Riem). Key concerns involve whether the media are attempting to offer an 'objective', 'accurate', 'balanced' and 'impartial' representation of the real world and whether there is equity in access to information and knowledge. Though these values may remain contested, there are independent criteria in terms of which rational argument can be conducted and better educated judgements arrived at.[34] Has evidence ignored significant detail; has interviewing been prejudicial to a full and fair expression of opinion; have claims about causation been substantiated; have groups been spoken about in a pejorative way?

But, again, we are not concerned here with television as a work of art: for the practice of broadcasting as a form of journalism is wedded to the more neutral quality of the rhythm and diction and imagery of an informative, expository or argumentative style, and this 'serious' style imposes tight aesthetic limitations. The quality of aesthetic representation may reinforce enjoyment of this type of programming, as for instance viewers come to admire a particular presenter's skills or the well-crafted way in which news or documentary narrative is constructed, with, for instance, strong characters and plot or the insertion of brief, dramatic scenes and creative use of screen space. Stephen Lambert's *True Brits*, an examination of the inner workings of the Foreign Office, remains a classic instance of this blending of aesthetic sensibility into documentary reporting, but with aesthetic values the servant of a documentary purpose. Indeed, it is precisely in this way that attentive audiences can be delivered.

More seriously, however, consequent on the increasing commercialization of broadcasting, the characteristics of popular culture programming (like personalized and sensationalized storytelling and reliance on vividness and immediacy) have shown signs of becoming more influential as news broadcasters and documentary makers seek to attract and hold audiences. Drama documentaries, documentary dramas and 'fly-on-the-wall' investigative programmes have been developed as means of escape from these limitations on discourse. In effect, television journalism becomes concerned with entertaining, with telling a good story, and is assimilated into the practices of commercial news production.[35] News is then a product whose qualities are defined by the business manager rather than the professional journalist. But the constraint on this influence remains the risk that pursuit of news, documentary and education strategies based on popular culture programme values will erode the authority on which such programmes ultimately depend. That authority is expressed in the form of a controlled, print-derived narrative structure with an emphasis on precise discourse and rigorous analysis rooted in careful research and techniques that emphasize the observational mode and exposition.[36] It derives, in the final analysis, from fundamental ethical principles governing the provision and dissemination of information and knowledge to citizens in a civilized, democratic society, as Hoffmann-Riem's chapter stresses; and from respect for the values of a literary culture.

Television as aesthetic experience

The third kind of experience offered by television is *aesthetic*. In contrast to the 'pleasure' values of entertainment and the 'instructional' values of news, current affairs and documentaries, television offers a third dimension – aesthetic experience. It provides moments of 'delight' by composing memorable and striking images that provoke a contemplative attitude in the viewer. Here television approximates to Aristotle's 'poetics'. We turn to it, like we turn to other arts, for a fuller, *contemplative* realization of the often terrible and pitiful, sometimes just poignant, condition of human life, putting that condition in its cosmic setting, educating our thoughts and feelings and broadening our sympathies.[37] It is not a matter of art being didactic; indeed, art is likely to question convention and suggest that the making of moral judgements is difficult. Art clarifies some aspect of private or public morality in a vivid way. It leaves a philosophical residue in the mind. Life, in the form of a subject matter and of the materials of art, is delicately moulded into a shape. The values of physical action and location do not impose themselves either; they are there, along with dialogue, to illustrate the complexities of characterization.

For Aristotle, poetics was very much the preserve of the dramatic arts, and on television drama has been very much the epicentre of the aesthetic dimension of its activities. 'One-off' television drama and drama series have been *par excellence* the arena in which it has been possible to engage most creatively in the activity of imagining, making and moving about among verbal, pictorial and musical images: in which viewers have had the 'poetic' character of television revealed to them.[38] They can contemplate with delight the painstakingly detailed and yet unified *mise-en-scène* as high-quality materials of language, gesture, set design, costume, lighting, screen space and music are imaginatively composed into an expressive whole.

As an art form television drama is distinctive and demanding in the scale of collaboration required among diverse artisans and artists: the playwright, actors, set/costume/lighting designers, camerapeople, make-up artists, composers, musicians and directors. It is an activity of putting together literary values (of plotting, characterization and dialogue) with visual values and musical values, in such a way that the narrative structure is enriched and reinforced. But the basis of this collective achievement remains the strength of the authorial voice: in short, its roots in, and respect for, the values of a literary culture. The art form of television drama has produced a series of 'name' British authors for the medium: sometimes as adapters (like Andrew Davies for George Eliot's *Middlemarch* and Angus Wilson's *Anglo-Saxon Attitudes*), sometimes as original scriptwriters (for instance, Alan Bleasdale, Alan Bennett, Trevor Griffiths, Mike Leigh, Peter Nichols and Dennis Potter). These writers have had to navigate the complex and difficult relationship between television and literature. The aesthetic quality of their work derives from the strength of their authorial voice: the way in which they reveal themselves in the style of their work. They treat their audiences with respect by providing an intelligent and sensitive portrayal of the human condition. Literature has provided established narratives, powered by the distinctiveness of an original imagination, moral intelligence and language, strong in structure, 'round' in characterization and rich in diction and meanings. From this source have come such 'jewels in the crown' of television as Eliot's *Middlemarch*, Jane Austen's *Persuasion*, and Charles Dickens's *Hard Times* and *Martin Chuzzlewit*, the product of creative adaptations that involve a sophisticated capacity for retelling and remaking narratives.[39] This kind of creative adaptation is one, and arguably not the most important, relationship between television and literature. Television's role in creatively exploiting original scriptwriting, like Potter's *The Singing Detective*, Trevor Griffiths's *Hope in the Year Two*, Edgar Reitz's 11-part series *Heimat* or Jurek Becker's *Liebling Kreuzberg* and *Wir Sind Auch Nur Ein Volk* is crucial if originality is to be sustained in its cultural role and if television is to draw aesthetic strength from, and support, a literary culture.

At the same time, television scriptwriting must be consistent with – and draw strength out of – the technical constraints of the medium: for instance, its intimacy and the scope that it offers for subtle acting performance, exemplified beautifully in Bennett's series *Talking Heads*. In essence, *Talking Heads* represents the way in which technology of television can be subordinated to a literary purpose. The other extreme of 'writing to picture' is more a feature of popular culture entertainment programmes in which a strong authorial voice gives way to the visual and sound values of action and special effects as means of dramatic representation. More characteristic of television drama as an art form is the attempt to fuse literary, sound and visual values into a coherent whole of expressive portrayal that serves to delight and engage audiences in a special way. Examples from Britain in the 1980s include *Edge of Darkness* and *The Jewel in the Crown*, and from Germany Rainer Fassbinder's *Berlin Alexanderplatz* (1979). It is precisely this experience of delight – of participating in an exceptional experience of rich imagery, inviting patient and involved viewing – that marks out the works of art in television drama as landmarks in the history of television.

In making an overall assessment of television as an aesthetic experience some qualifications are in order. Heuristically, the distinction between these three very different forms of engagement in television as a cultural form is valuable in offsetting attempts to generalize about television as though it were a homogeneous medium. It also challenges the view that the content and form of the medium is simply technologically determined. In fact, the complexity of the medium is even greater than the distinction between these three modes of experience suggests. Genres interact with each other: entertainment with news coverage, for instance. Though aesthetic values are most strongly represented in television drama, not all – or even most – television drama can claim to be works of art. Such objects are the exception. Moreover, aesthetic values can gain a substantial foothold in unreservedly entertainment programmes: in a detective series like *Inspector Morse*, for instance, with its languid panning shots of Oxford, brilliant pastiche music and use of 'name' authors like Peter Nichols and prestigious actors. They are also represented in the work of documentary makers like Stephen Lambert. The results are classics of their genre that are able to engage their audiences in contemplation. They show that aesthetic values can be mobile across genres, capable of giving a special character and status to a detective story or a documentary, lifting it beyond the conventions of its genre into the status of a work of art. It is when the materials of television, on the one hand, and a significant subject matter, on the other, have been transfigured into a coherent expressive portrayal that we can recognize the work of art. Television drama, whether 'one-off' or in serial form, is simply the most likely genre for this achievement.

From television to multimedia: the discourse about standards and the pervasiveness of politics

As was noted at the beginning of this chapter, we need to be alert to the context that surrounds the use of words like culture and to be sensitive to who is winning the war of words over standards. A key question, then, is who is dominating this discourse, and why. Answering this question will awake us to the pervasiveness of politics, even where discourse appears at its most technical. As we shall see below, the technological, economic and political contexts of broadcasting are in a process of radical alteration. In the period 1995–97 alone it is estimated that Britain could have twelve new terrestrial television channels, whilst Europe will have more than 500 new satellite channels. These developments derive from the digital revolution. They make possible not just a vast increase of channels but also new services: like 'near video-on-demand', with the start time of films being staggered with brief intervals; 'multiplexing', as the same programmes are repeated in different order across several channels to offer greater viewing choice; more premium subscription channels; and, eventually, 'pay-per-view'.

The discourse about literary culture

Traditionally, in Western Europe discourse about cultural standards has been dominated by the élites of the public service broadcasting institutions, like the BBC. In essence, they justified their monopoly or privileged position by reference to their special mission in promoting and safeguarding cultural standards. Closed or tightly controlled access to broadcasting and the licence fee were designed as instruments to underpin this mission: to keep commercial and political pressures at a distance from programme making. Within that protected framework aesthetic and ethical standards could flourish. Over time their definition altered: the shift from 'detached' news reporting to embrace intrusive forms of investigative journalism, for example. But the discourse of broadcasting management was dominated by individuals whose intellectual roots and commitments were to the values of a literary culture: upholding the integrity of broadcasting journalism and the aesthetic standards of television drama and its cultural role in relaying the arts (BBC's Radio 3 being a model in relation to music). The discourse within public service broadcasting integrated within the medium the values of a literary culture that it had threatened to destroy. It emulated the modes of a print-based discourse, emphasizing precise language, sharp analysis and detachment. Director-generals of the BBC, from Lord Reith to Alasdair Milne, symbolized the priority attached to this mode of discourse.

Even so, long before the advent of new media like cable and satellite television or the age of 'multimedia', this discourse was beset by tensions and contradictions. First, critics were quick to condemn the inconsistencies that came to characterize programming policy consequent on the tensions between the discourse of public service broadcasting and the pressures of the real and ever-changing world that it served and on which it drew for its subject matter and materials. In practice, broadcasting had to reflect as well as lead society, to earn its licence fee by attracting and holding viewers and to bear in mind the continuing need for broad public support. The discourse of public service broadcasting represented the victory of an élite committed to the values of a literary culture. But it had to relate to, and gain support from within, a society in which consumer values were increasingly ascendant, with rising material affluence, in which leisure time was growing, and in which a combination of demographic and economic factors made youth culture a new phenomenon. The result was an emerging gap between the established discourse and the reality of programming, with, from 1967, BBC's Radio 1 pioneering a pop music format rooted firmly in the values of oral culture. Even earlier, from 1954, the BBC had been faced with the challenge of whether and how to adapt its programming to the advent of commercial television in the form of ITV. Hence, well before new media competitors like Rupert Murdoch came on the scene or the potential of new information and communication technologies had been fully appreciated, critics could point to the standards of public service broadcasting as a myth, laid bare by the realities of competitive scheduling in the search to improve ratings. With the arrival of new technologies it became possible to argue that this myth was now best consigned to oblivion. The error in this argument came from the failure to see that such inconsistencies were in fact symptomatic of public service broadcasting's 'amazing trick', the trick by which it rebuilds itself in a context in which broadcasting is necessarily socially and historically constituted. The problem is not the insubstantiality of its standards; it is how to ensure that they continue to be promoted as broadcasting reconstitutes itself.

Secondly, the élite wedded to the values of literary culture that dominated the discourse of public service broadcasting was itself far from homogeneous. Indeed, it was beset by its own tensions: between those who were identified with 'tradition' and those identified with 'experiment' in the arts; between those who propagated an elitist conception that denigrated the values of popular culture and those who sought to embrace the subject matter and audiences of popular culture in more challenging contemplative or instructive programmes; and between advocates of detached news and current affairs reporting and advocates of investigative journalism. There was, in short, an ongoing internal debate within traditional public service broadcasting about how its cultural mission should be defined. There were those who wanted to conceive that mission in less remote and aloof terms; there were others who complained that standards of taste and behaviour were being sacrificed. Disenchantment within the broad coalition of discourse supporting public service broadcasting was not simply a child of the 1980s and 1990s.

These tensions underline the pervasiveness of politics in the traditional discourse about public service broadcasting, whatever the rhetoric about its being outside or above politics. The profound change of discourse in the 1980s and 1990s reflected a shift in the nature of the groups dominating the war of words about broadcasting. The values of literary culture associated with the traditional

broadcasting élites and their programme philosophy were marginalized as these groups were put on the defensive by 'engaged'
technologists, by the increased professional self-confidence of *homo
economicus*, and by the modernizing ambitions of political and
administrative élites in the face of economic crisis. The discourses
of these three groups have interacted to redefine broadcasting
in industrial and commercial terms and drive issues of aesthetic
and ethical standards away from the centre of the agenda. These
discourses deserve more detailed attention. Collectively, as we have
noted, their victory was assisted by the legacy of the inherited tensions
and inconsistencies besetting public service broadcasting.

The discourse of science

The practical innovating activities of electrical engineers were
catalysts for far-reaching changes in the discourse of broadcasting.
Microprocessors, electronic imaging, cable and satellite represented
a cluster of interacting innovations that constituted a communications revolution – the so-called digital revolution. With the gathering
whirlwind of new technological artefacts every aspect of the television
production process was affected: from camera work to film and
sound editing. So too was the process of media use: with the shift from
more passive viewer reception via the 'dumb' television to interactive
usage via the 'intelligent' computer.

The discourse of this world of digital communication embraced the
new vocabulary of 'convergence', 'information superhighways' and
'multimedia' into a new vision of a media. 'Convergence' meant that
the traditional boundaries between broadcasting, telecommunications, computing, film and print had become irrelevant. It legitimated
the entry, and role of, new non-broadcasting actors in broadcasting
discourse. Quite simply, all forms of information, whether written
words, sounds or pictures, can be transmitted as a stream of numbers
(rather than via differing analogues). They can thus be mixed as
never before. 'Information superhighways' refers to the 'broad-band'
communication networks, using fibre-optic cable, satellite and digital
compression, to carry a vast new range of audio-visual services.
This development removed a part of the rationale for public service
broadcasting monopoly or privileging: the constraint of spectrum
scarcity. It legitimated the assimilation of broadcasting into a
competitive media market, as simply a form of 'electronic publishing'.

'Multimedia' meant that the individual could simultaneously access and manipulate, via a personal monitor, all kinds of information – textual, graphics, sound, pictures and video – drawing on the apparently limitless number-carrying capacity of the 'information super-highway'. Each person could pick the information that they wanted in the form they wanted (e.g. choosing 'bullet points' over prose style), devise their own programmes, make up their own programme schedule, and interact immediately with and interrogate the supplier. The visionaries of 'multimedia', led by Nicholas Negroponte of MIT, were in effect legitimating the media consumer as king and the creation of vast markets for new 'on-line' multimedia products: from video-on-demand, 'on-line' news services, interactive education and training, 'virtual' tele-shopping and point-of-sale promotions, to interactive games and desktop video-conferencing.[40]

As Lübbe and Schulze argue in this volume, they failed to address the ethical issues that were raised about media use; and, following the arguments in the chapters by Hoffmann-Riem and Winterhoff-Spurk, they were mistaken in thinking that ethical issues about media production had become irrelevant. The same errors attended the neglect of aesthetic standards. They were a consequence of the way in which media discourse had become defined in terms of the vocabularies of computing and telecommunications. The more thoughtful industry practitioners were aware that the central challenge was to treat the new medium on its own terms: that its main potential did not lie in simply trying to use it as a new way of relaying existing media products like books, magazines and television programmes: and that hence the key actors were 'the organizers of the creative process', the 'programmers'.[41] But simply to criticize the marginalization of the programmers in the radical transformation to 'multimedia' as commercially mistaken does not go far enough. It does not come to grips with the issues of aesthetic and ethical standards.

In an immediate and obvious sense the context of the new discourse was provided by the scientific paradigm, giving an 'objective' character and source of 'authority' to the changes in progress. But, on closer inspection, this new discursive system about new media rests on a bedrock of narrow and arid assumptions, in particular a political faith in the ultimate benefits of science as a guide to action. The fundamental problem is that such a paradigm has, in fact, nothing adequate to say on questions of aesthetic and ethical standards in broadcasting. Its rationality is essentially instrumental: a celebration of what Arnold called 'faith in machinery'. This constraint does not, and indeed should not, prevent technologists from spelling out what they see as the implications of technological changes – for instance, the shift from 'mass' media to 'personal' media. Their aesthetic and ethical judgements about the value and use of these technological changes do not, however, derive any special authority from their scientific expertise. Aesthetic and ethical standards cannot simply be constructed by applying the scientific paradigm. The source of deepest concern comes from the possibility that, in practice, the social and political prestige of the scientific paradigm may be such that, erroneously, it may be accepted as having such an authority.

The discourse of economics

The rise of *homo economicus* in broadcasting, as in other sectors, was one of the major political phenomena of the 1980s. In broadcasting it was represented by the rise to power of a new breed of professionally trained managers and accountants, concentrating on mapping out corporate strategies, designing market-research-based approaches and putting financial control systems in place. An example was provided by the efficiency-oriented discourse of John Birt as director-general of the BBC after 1992 (and deputy director-general since 1987), with its 'downsizing' and 'producer choice'. This change of discourse was primarily externally-driven. It responded to the new statutory requirement in the Broadcasting Act of 1990 that, by 1993 at the latest, at least 25 per cent of BBC as well as ITV programmes must be commissioned from independent producers: a political attempt to stimulate the growth of what was seen as a leaner, more efficient programme production sector. Also, and more crucially, the efficiency-oriented discourse was designed to head off political resistance to the renewal of the BBC's charter in 1997 and to its continued financing by means of the licence fee. In the White Paper *The Future of the BBC – Serving the Nation, Competing Worldwide* of July 1994, which demonstrated that this change of discourse had been successful in achieving these objectives, the government expressed its hope that the BBC would 'evolve into an international multimedia enterprise', while maintaining its primary role as public service broadcaster to the UK. The key internal innovation in April 1993 was 'producer choice'.[42] Under this new system of internal pricing BBC services had to compete with external providers for business from the BBC's own producers.

Though the driving force was economic efficiency, the underlying market paradigm of competition and choice did not in fact completely govern the internal discourse of the BBC. Much of it was tailored for external consumption, to persuade politicians that the BBC was not complacent. Even then, its documents revealed just how troubled it was about its role: recognizing, on the one hand, that it needed to be more market-research-based, providing specialized programming for more fragmented audiences, but, on the other, still concerned to 'speak to the nation' with popular programmes that brought together genuinely national audiences with creative talent.[43]

Far more unequivocally expressive of a discourse based on the market paradigm of classical economics was the vision of broadcasting as merely subsumed in an 'electronic publishing market', expressed in the Peacock Committee report of May 1986 on financing the BBC. In such a context the licence fee could no longer be justified: subscription and 'pay-per-view' were more desirable mechanisms of finance. Within this economic paradigm broadcasting was no longer seen as a public or social good. It was a private transaction between viewer and broadcaster, akin to that to be found in the publishing industry. Programmes constituted leisure or luxury goods; hence neither public service provision nor extensive public regulation was desirable. The simple objective of broadcasting, as of media in general, was to maximize consumer welfare: and this objective was to be met by promoting competition and choice and financing by subscription and by 'pay-per-view'.[44]

The context of this discursive system of the competitive market was again essentially political: in this case the moral agenda of liberalism, of privileging individual choice and self-interest over communitarian ideas of public interest. The strength of this agenda derived from its association with the rise to political power of the middle classes that displaced more traditional patrician élites and associated with figures like Margaret Thatcher in Britain and Silvio Berlusconi in Italy. It was both instinctive and rational for the middle classes to identify with the values of individual competition and choice. Acting as the ideologists of these classes, economists argued that self-interest and personal aggrandizement would maximize public advancement. Professional economists with their market paradigm played, accordingly, a central role in transforming media discourse.

Most seriously of all, the market paradigm, like the scientific paradigm, evicts issues of aesthetic and ethical standards by reducing them to matters of personal taste. It has no means of distinguishing between the claims of the 'best self' and the 'ordinary self'. It celebrates the freedom to say and do just what we like and ignores aesthetic and ethical standards in terms of which we can experience internal growth and the education of a discriminating taste. In this respect it is responsible for a narrow and arid discourse in media.

The discourse of competitiveness

But, perhaps most fundamentally, the impacts of the scientific and market paradigms on media discourse gained their inspiration and momentum from a broader-based change in political discourse at the level of political parties, parliaments and political executives. From the 1970s onwards, predating the emergence of 'multimedia', political discourse at this level began to shift from a consensus around the managed economy and the welfare state to problems of international competitiveness. The process took a different form in the various Western states and proceeded at contrasting rates, with economic crisis as the main catalyst for change: for Britain the turning point was 1975–76, for France 1982–83. This new attachment to the values of the 'competitive state' had its roots in deep structural changes within the international political economy. Structural change took two main forms: a displacement of manufacturing to newly industrializing countries, and a shift in employment in advanced industrial countries from manufacturing to services. The consequences were fundamental: including an erosion of the traditional strong class solidarity on which the political left had been based, a new political salience for service industries, pressure for more flexible labour markets and, not least, a new prestige of liberal market economics. Competitiveness meant modernization in the form of revitalizing old sectors and developing new sectors.

Broadcasting was inextricably caught up in this process of change in political discourse: in the general sense of urgency about developing the service sector of which it was a part, in the consequent excitement about new sectors like 'multimedia', and in the significance attributed to 'information superhighways' as the networks of the future. The language of the new technologies was co-opted into the extraordinary renaissance of economic liberalism. In consequence of the new 'market imperialism', a whole range of public goods – like broadcasting – were 'commodified'.[45] The political agenda shifted to deregulation and privatization, with more or less difficulty depending on domestic institutional factors.[46] Centre-right governments were, ideologically, the most natural vehicles for this new discourse on the competitive state and the most likely beneficiaries. There was, not least, a particular political advantage in subsuming their rhetoric of competitiveness into their traditional political vision of making their countries 'strong again'.

The discourse about industrial structure and regulation for multimedia

Despite the displacement of the discourse of literary culture by the discursive systems of the science and market paradigms, the coalition of interests that supported 'multimedia' were themselves beset by tensions. The constant pace of technological innovations, like digital compression, unsettled commercial and political judgements. At one level the issue was straightforward: who would come up with the 'killer applications' that would enable these technologies to be effectively exploited in the market-place. The torturing questions were: what were these 'killer applications', and how were they to be created? In the creative combination of text (say poetry), music and pictures were new opportunities for aesthetic expression; whilst hypertext provided an entry into new possibilities for developing expository and argumentative styles in education and journalism. But the question remained of the extent to which multimedia should focus on relaying existing art forms (like collections of art galleries or productions of symphonies) or whether it must develop its own forms of aesthetic expression as a distinctive medium.

More immediately difficult was the question of the implications for industry structure. One implication did at least seem clear. The key structural change was that, in a more competitive market-place, the cost of delivery of programmes and information was likely to fall relative to content. This change was to the disadvantage of broadcasters and network providers. The beneficiaries would be the programme makers – the studios (like Disney), the software companies (like Microsoft) and the information providers (like

Reuters). They could provide the broad range of applications without which 'multimedia' and 'information superhighways' have no future.

Beyond this level of agreement the implications seemed less clear-cut. Technologists tended to think in terms of vertical integration, of companies extending via merger and joint venture to embrace both hardware and software: network operation and consumer electronics, on the one hand, and programme provision, on the other. In this way it would be possible to take advantage of the 'logic of convergence' and exploit synergies between consumer electronics, computer software, books, newspapers, film, cable television, telecommunications and broadcasting networks. Examples included the link-up between Rupert Murdoch's News Corporation (already incorporating Fox Broadcasting and Twentieth Century Fox) and the telecommunications giant MCI; Disney and AT&T, the largest long-distance telecommunications operator in the United States; Disney's acquisition of Capital Cities/ABC, the American broadcasting group; Viacom's purchase of Paramount Communications and the publishers Simon & Schuster; the creation of Time-Warner in 1989, US West's stake in Time-Warner and Time-Warner's offer for Turner Broadcasting System; Sony's acquisition of Columbia Pictures and Matsushita's of Universal; Microsoft and Dream Works, the film, television and multimedia joint venture created by Stephen Spielberg, former Disney chief Jeffrey Katzenberg and the music impresario David Geffen; Pearson's purchase of Software Toolworks and Grundy Worldwide and marriage with Mindscape; and the consortia based on British Telecom, Deutsche Telekom and France Telecom in order to develop 'video-on-demand'.[47] But such deals were fraught with difficulties, not least of marrying together the very different corporate cultures of consumer electronics and film companies and of telecommunications and cable companies.[48] An indication of the difficulties in realizing the development of 'multimedia' and 'information superhighways' in the United States came in early 1994 when the proposed merger of Bell Atlantic and Telecommunications Inc. (TCI) and the proposed stake of Southwestern Bell in Cox Enterprises were called off.

Corporate management literature and micro-economic analysis yielded different conclusions about appropriate industrial structure for the age of multimedia. In one view, technological 'convergence' created an inbuilt advantage for the company that could control all key aspects of the industry and use corporate strategy to integrate and transform its operations. The crucial commercial requirement was to move pre-emptively to forge alliances before others did. In another view, the advantage rested with a contrasting approach. Given the highly complex set of overlapping markets being created by these technological changes, corporate actors were most likely to benefit by developing distinct 'niche' roles based on the imaginative use of their real capabilities rather than of their financial assets – the managerial principle of 'sticking to the knitting'. If Viacom represented the former approach, Microsoft and Turner Entertainment had pursued the latter. But by 1995 they too were being caught up in the merger mania sweeping the media industry.

To the tension between technological discourse and market and industrial realities was added a tension about the appropriate role and objectives of regulatory policy for this new industry. The new technological and market-based discourse about broadcasting and multimedia could agree on the appropriateness of 'light-touch' regulation to promote technical innovation and economic competition and choice. The British Cable and Broadcasting Act of 1984 and the Broadcasting Act of 1990 exemplified this shift in the discourse of regulation. But the question remained – how was that regulatory role to be defined? Was the regulator to encourage as much domestic competition as possible to enlarge consumer choice? The appropriate regulatory tool for that objective was to set limits on any major corporate actor's 'share of voice', both in the total media market and in each market segment. A body like the Office of Fair Trading would need strengthening to enable it to implement tough competition policies. This approach was taken by the British Screen Advisory Council, the all-industry body set up to advise the governmment on the television, film and video industries. Or was the objective of regulation to ensure that internationally competitive media companies could emerge, as advocated by Carlton Communications? In that case the appropriate regulatory tool was an easing of rules on cross-media and broadcasting ownership to encourage takeover activity and merger.

Regulatory policy tended to hover uneasily between these positions. On the one hand, the formation of the Granada/London Weekend Television and Carlton/Central groups illustrated the process of easing rules on broadcasting ownership in British ITV; on the other, in 1995 the British government was suggesting, to the immense anger of Rupert Murdoch, a 20 per cent ownership ceiling in each media segment. Indicative of Germany's regulatory problems was the inability to agree to act against the Kirch family holdings (in Sat1 and Pro 7) despite a regulatory restriction on owning more than 25 per cent in more than one channel. In France the Balladur government relaxed the 25 per cent restriction on ownership in television companies. Promptly, the building group Bouygues substantially increased its ownership share in TF1; the interlocked Compagnie Générale des Eaux (CGE), Havas and France Telecom gained a controlling position in the subscription channel Canal Plus; and Lyonnaise des Eaux and CLT of Luxembourg strengthened their stakes in M6. These cases were indicative of the way in which the conflictual discourse of broadcasting regulation (fostering competition versus building internationally competitive media groups) camouflaged 'insider' political links, protecting the corporate interests of players like Kirch, Bouygues, CGE and Lyonnaise des Eaux. This pervasiveness of politics in discourse on regulation did not, however, reduce regulation to inescapably partisan perspectives. There remained a public interest rationale for regulation, defined in terms of rights of citizens in the media and accountability of corporate actors.

A second question was prompted by 'convergence' which challenged the traditional boundaries of regulatory control. Was it satisfactory to continue with an independent regulation of television (as by the British Independent Television Commission), of print advertising and of telephone information services? Or was a comprehensive media regulatory commission required? Conflicting positions on this issue reflected the desire of some actors to protect the special status of television and the objective of others to have it seen as just another 'media segment'. Again, though partisan perspectives were inescapable, the public interest rationale for regulation had a solid basis in the objective of ensuring that operators were not able to subvert regulatory controls by exploiting uncertainties about jurisdictional boundaries and differences of regulatory approach in different sectors.

But these regulatory questions faded into second place behind the fundamental question of rules on 'conditional access'. Central here was the issue of the kind of encryption standard that should determine customer access to the new subscription digital broadcast services. This issue was essentially about who drives the emerging market-place. On the one hand, there were those – led by BSkyB and its leading shareholder, Murdoch's News International – who were driving the new market (20 per cent of the channels on the three Astra digital satellites due by 1997 were expected to be operated by Murdoch). Their objective was to protect their market leadership position; their preferred common standard was simulcrypt, decoders with one slot for a proprietary smart card. On the other hand, those whose entry into the new market-place was slower and more hesitant favoured multicrypt, decoders with two or more slots, allowing a variety of access systems to prevent monopoly. Public service broadcasters in particular feared being marginalized in the digital revolution, perhaps being squeezed out altogether: not just in the huge new digital satellite capacity but also in the new terrestrial digital capacity. Though by March 1995 a compromise European common standard had been agreed on a two-tier conditional access system enabling either simulcrypt or multicrypt, this agreement did not resolve the key regulatory problem: how to prevent one actor – notably News Corporation – dominating access. Even a former News International figure like Andrew Neil could ask whether regulation was needed to enshrine rights to open access on fair terms for service providers; to published tariffs applicable to all on the same basis; to a full and public explanation when access is denied; to a legal requirement not to discriminate in favour or against any provider; and to independent and binding arbitration when there is a dispute.[49] In June 1995 the European Parliament advocated precisely these rights. But, though such rights go some way towards facing up to the ethical issues raised by the digital revolution, they ignore the dimension of aesthetic standards and how these standards are to be retained – and strengthened.

Rediscovering a passion for standards

However great, fascinating and pregnant with consequences may be the internal tensions and conflicts about corporate strategy and regulatory policy among the enthusiasts for the digital revolution, it is clear that the war of words about broadcasting is being won by voices that have little, if any, serious commitment to the values of a literary culture. The driving ideas behind the shift in discourse have been a technocratic 'faith in machinery' and a liberal faith in our freedom to do and say as we please: in short, to be enabled to be our 'ordinary selves', immersed in the practical world of our pleasures, of satisfying our desires. The individual consumer is pictured as sovereign, with her/his tastes the arbiter of what services will be provided. Increased leisure time and greater economic affluence for the large majority have combined with new technologies, and the specific characteristics of television ('immediacy', 'liveness', 'dramatic representation'), to open up vast new opportunities to indulge our pleasures. And, as we have seen, pleasure is not to be regarded as valueless. Relaxation, escapism and excitement are not to be dismissed as trivial, banal or worthless activities. Equally, programmes that satisfy these desires – from advertisements to quiz shows – are not to be celebrated as art forms, in postmodern style. Such celebration rests on a confusion of quite different activities: of the practical activity of satisfying particular desires (to relax, to escape, to be excited) and the contemplative or poetic activity of delighting in making, observing, transforming and meditating upon images.[50]

The argument of this chapter is not that the poetic activity that we associate with aesthetic experience is somehow 'superior' to the practical activity of taking pleasure in being entertained by a comedian or talk show presenter; that the quality of an individual is to be judged by their avoidance of 'banal' and 'trivial' pleasures. Such snobbery rests on a view of man that neglects the importance of our sensory and sensual nature, and risks hypocrisy. Our pleasures are valuable, and if technology can better satisfy them we are gainers. Indeed, the precondition for a successful defence of standards is a recognition that broadcasting is historically and socially constituted; and that, with the 'digital revolution', its material nature is changing and will change. The question is how aesthetic and ethical standards are to be promoted within this new framework.

But – and the qualification is critical – we are ill served by the way in which the newly dominant voices in the discourse about broadcasting and multimedia have marginalized or dismissed the issue of aesthetic and ethical standards. The discursive systems of the scientific paradigm and the market paradigm have nothing much to say on this issue, either ignoring it or relativizing standards and reducing them to simply a subjective matter. Interestingly, as we saw in the introduction, internal academic developments in media studies have reinforced rather than countered this neglect of aesthetics and ethics. The danger is that, as our popular culture flourishes in the form of the 'cultural industries', organized as a lean market-oriented production process, so the quality of our common life will diminish. It will diminish if broadcasting loses sight of its other crucial task besides entertainment: namely, the liberation of the creative impulses of the artist in the service of aesthetic standards and the promotion of the ethical standards on which 'good' journalism is based. Impartiality continues to matter in news and current affairs programming irrespective of the number of providers: it matters because it represents a central standard of well-informed and civilized debate. Equally, the number of channels is secondary to the quality of images that are conveyed within the programmes on offer – 'round' characterization, vivid language, striking visual images. In short, broadcasting remains in the business of critical intelligence, of educating tastes, sensibilities and minds. The trick will be to reinvent this quality of its business as it 'shoots Niagara'.

The question is, then, how can that capability be sustained – and developed – in the context of such a vortex of change. We must begin by recognizing the extent to which broadcasting is socially and historically constituted; that its salvation must lie not in rejecting the digital revolution and multimedia but in cultivating the 'amazing trick' of reinventing itself. Realism involves not just taking change on board in this way but also recognizing that, even in the best of aesthetic and ethical worlds, the *vita contemplativa* is not on offer. We can only expect moments of contemplative delight in the endless restless flow of contrivance and curiosity that is broadcasting. We are perhaps always likely to look for it more than we find it.

But this kind of realism about the different modes of human experience and about technological and economic change is not enough. If we are to live in an aesthetically rich and ethically chal-lenging culture we need a passionate commitment to standards. In neither its aesthetic nor its ethical senses is culture simply a subjective matter of taste, of commending what one likes. Aesthetic judgement involves an appeal to certain independent criteria, admittedly general and open to interpretation, in terms of which it is possible to educate one's taste and make one's perceptions more sophisticated. It is not just emotivism or subjectivism at work. The question is how this passion for standards is to be cultivated in a context of televisual technology and dominant discursive paradigms that are displacing the values of literary culture. Who is likely to be most able to shift the centre of gravity in broadcasting back to a discourse that celebrates aesthetic and ethical values?

Three opportunities seem to present themselves: a shift of intellectual paradigm ushered in by change in educational practices; changes in regulatory strategy; and, possibly most promising of all, a redefinition of corporate strategy in the media sector.

Shift of intellectual paradigm?

By shift of intellectual paradigm I refer to a return to respect for the values of a literary culture: in schools, in higher education, in the media and throughout society. The prospects for this development do not seem very promising. As we have seen, television itself – never mind multimedia – has not been intrinsically hospitable as a medium to literary culture. Its disposition has been to reinvent the values of oral culture, utilizing the familiar verbal forms of gossip and direct address to encourage empathy with television personalities and 'bonding' with channels. And television has become the central cultural stage from which schoolchildren and university students derive their stock of meanings. The prime casualties have been the practice of fiction reading and reduced tolerance periods and tolerance levels. In schools and universities themselves, reflecting the wider social dominance of the televisual, literacy levels have shown no real signs of advance. As the great English social historian G. M. Trevelyan wrote, 'education has produced a vast population, able to read but unable to distinguish what is worth reading'. To take one indicator of literacy from a country, France, traditionally imagined to value literary culture: in 1974, 27 per cent of French homes had no books in them; in 1960 an opinion poll revealed that half the French never read a book.[51] Within higher education the traditional prestige of the intellectual values of critical literacy, in effect showing one how to read well, has given way to the more instrumental values of computer literacy and transferable skills. Perhaps most sadly of all, media studies is part of the problem rather than the solution. Its spectacular growth as measured in a rise of applications for media studies in British universities from 5,855 in 1990 to 32,862 in 1995 offers little comfort. In the grip of various forms of poststructuralism and postmodernism, views on cultural standards within media studies have tended to be subjectivist and relativist. The question of intellectual paradigm is in fact crucial for, in the long term, it shapes what we demand of media: and what we demand we are likely to get. Ultimately the answer lies in a return of educational practice to the

fostering of standards of critical literacy as ɩ
and computer texts as well as books; to a fosterin
aesthetic and ethical judgement; to an awareness
role in drawing out our 'best selves'.

Change of regulatory strategy?

The role of the regulator is the particular concern of the chapter by
Hoffmann-Riem. What is clear is that the huge expansion and
commercialization of broadcasting and the media sector as a whole
are exposing the enormous implementation problems that confront
state regulation in general. State actors have interests (investment,
jobs, taxes, prestige) in the expansion of the market; they are subject
to a process of regulatory arbitrage in increasingly internationalized
media markets that works to reduce regulatory costs and barriers;
and, accordingly, they are induced to work with key corporate
players.[52] The consequence is that the organization of self-regulation
among market players seems a more sensible strategy. But, as
Hoffmann-Riem stresses, there are ethical issues related to the fact
that viewers are citizens with rights to information and not just
consumers. Regulation must accordingly deal directly with issues
of market structure, notably access, with the objective of securing
citizenship rights at the centre of attention.

From the perspective of the theme of this chapter regulation needs
also to take on board the question of programme quality standards.
This question can be addressed in the framework of franchising
and monitoring of performance of companies in fulfilling their legal
obligations, as the Independent Television Commission sought to
do under the terms of the British Broadcasting Act of 1990. For
instance, in 1994 it sharply criticized the programme quality of the
new commercial breakfast television operator GMTV and the new
Carlton channel (pointing to a 'glib and superficial' series), while
praising Channel Four. Armed as the ITC was with the sanctions of
fines, shortening of licences and even their withdrawal, its criticisms
carried a certain weight. But the real constraints on the exercise of
its authority were visible in the way in which it was persuaded to
lighten the licence obligations of GMTV, notably in relation to news
and current affairs.

Arguably far more crucial is the role of the regulator in ensuring
that broadcasting companies are adequately financed for the purpose

suing creative programme making, even if buying in from independent producers. The precondition – though certainly not the guarantee – of aesthetically excellent programme making and the adequate pursuit of the highest ethical standards in journalism is a solid financial basis for the major players.[53] As with the 1990 Broadcasting Act, with its principle of competitive tendering for commercial broadcasting licences (subject to a 'quality threshold'), the regulatory framework can be inhospitable to quality broadcasting. The result is a siphoning of resources from programme making to the Treasury. A similar effect is produced in public service broadcasting, as with the BBC, by political moves to restrict increases in the licence fee in a period of mounting competition. France, however, is illustrative of the failures that follow if the objective of encouraging media investment by financially powerful companies is pursued without reference to the real capabilities of these companies in media. The financial power of the building giant Bouygues and civil engineering groups like CGE and Lyonnaise des Eaux is no guarantee of improved programme standards.

Redefinition of corporate strategy? 'Market takers' and 'market makers'

If the prospects for a shift of intellectual paradigm back to a respect for the values of literary culture do not seem promising, and if regulation appears beset with practical implementation problems in the face of market pressures, there is still a third possibility. This possibility stems from the corporate self-interests of media corporations. Media corporations face a choice about market and corporate strategy. On the one hand, they can be 'market takers'. They can seek commercial success by making products 'for the market'. The consequence for corporate strategy is a ratings-based approach to programme scheduling and making; and for the programme production process a 'formula' approach. Reliance is placed on expensive data collection about what audiences appear to want and on the use of the latest business school techniques to systematically organize the production process (cost centres, internal pricing). Associated with this approach to corporate strategy is a disposition to recommission 'proven' successes, a shift of corporate power to professional managers dedicated to values and skills of market research and driven by performance yardsticks of financial performance. A higher premium is placed on the generic skills of accountants, market researchers and business consultants than on the 'industry-specific' creative skills of producers, writers and directors.

The alternative corporate approach is for the media company to seek to be a 'market maker'. 'Market making' involves seeking out creative individuals, programme makers and producers, whose talents reside in an imaginative grasp of the potential of their activities: who are not afraid to listen to their 'inner voice'. These companies know that they are in the difficult and special 'business of making culture'. A classic example was provided in the United States by MTM Enterprises under Grant Tinker in the 1970s and the legacy of creative talent that it spun off across American television (responsible, for instance, for *Hill Street Blues*, *St Elsewhere* and *Northern Exposure*). Its company secret lay in a certain kind of relationship between executives and producers, characterized by maximum support and 'minimal involvement', in employing the best people and then letting them get on with it.[54] Out of the experience of MTM came the new idea of 'quality demographics', of pursuing quality programme production for minority audiences that could nevertheless be desirable to advertisers. Channel Four in Britain exemplified a similar highly successful type of approach, with David Rose as senior commissioning editor for fiction being given full support by Jeremy Isaacs to develop television drama and particularly *Film on Four*. Interestingly, this type of strategic approach has been more successfully pioneered by the smaller newcomers than by the established broadcasting companies. On the other hand, Denis Forman and David Plowright as chairmen of Granada Television showed how, once a tradition of combining managerial flair with a passionate commitment to the aesthetics of programme making was established, it could be sustained. Granada was responsible for such works of television dramatic art as *Brideshead Revisited* and *The Jewel in the Crown*.

'Market makers' build around the skills of creative artists, providing a climate that encourages boldness in content and style; go for lean management systems, enabling producers to buy and commission without months of meetings with executives; see management as a process of facilitative support from accountants and market research specialists for the exercise of these creative skills (rather than vice versa); create space for experiment with new programme making (say one-off dramas), within a clear framework of budget and time constraints; recognize a 'right to fail' in programme production and use it as a learning experience; and judge performance on the basis of the most effective use of these 'real capabilities' of the company. They are on the whole sceptical of the claims of vertical integration and see the function of corporate planning and financial control as being to facilitate and support creative programme making. In that kind of corporate context entrepreneurial values can be the handmaiden of aesthetic and ethical values.

The future of quality television in the emerging age of the digital revolution hinges on how companies respond to the key structural development in the media market. Crucially, the biggest commercial opportunities face the programme makers rather than the network providers. Hence the main beneficiaries are likely to be the studios, the software companies and the information/news providers. Those companies that are most successful in liberating the creative skills of programme makers for the age of digital television and multimedia will be the big winners. But one must beware of a naïve optimism in the role of 'market makers' as the saviours of quality. The victory of 'market makers' is not guaranteed. The question of who controls the emerging markets remains open. By establishing financially and technologically dominant positions, certain companies which lack a driving passion for aesthetic values and ethical considerations may squeeze out creativity and innovation in programme making. Whether that kind of dominance is sustainable in the longer term is another matter. Small, quick-witted 'market makers', committed passionately to professional journalistic and aesthetic values, will continue to have the capability to inflict embarrassment and damage on conservative 'market takers'. And control of the networks will amount to little if the content is repetitive, predictable and boring. Content, not technology, is the emerging frontier of multimedia. The key battlefields will move from control of technology to issues of content.

This modest note of optimism about the potential within the corporate sector for 'market makers' to re-engage in the battle for aesthetic and journalistic values could be transformed into something more positive if public policy and educators were to seek more passionately to create a context in which the values of poetic imagery and journalistic integrity could thrive. Public policy is poorly equipped directly to pick out and support the 'market makers'. It can at least do so indirectly by taking up firm positions on 'shares of voice' in the media market as a whole and in different segments and in ensuring open and fair access to the new networks. More crucially, it must work with educators to foster the values of critical literacy, to create a growing demand for the highest aesthetic and ethical standards in cultural life. That change of climate can only work if educators themselves have a greater passion for these values than they have simply for the freedom to say and do just what we like or for a 'faith in machinery'. The *trahison des clercs* has taken the form of an intellectual preoccupation with the instrumental values of computer literacy and the relativism and subjectivism of variants of 'poststructuralism'. The route out of this loss of intellectual confidence is a return to the recognition that culture teaches us that we have a 'best self' as well as an 'ordinary self'; that we can educate and improve our tastes; that culture is an activity of discrimination; and that we must re-engage with normative debates about aesthetic and ethical standards if our powers of perception are to be strengthened.

References

1. M. Weitz, *Problems in Aesthetics*, London: Macmillan, 1959.
2. See, respectively, A. Gray and J. McGuigan (eds), *Studying Culture: An Introductory Reader*, London: Edward Arnold, 1993, p. ix; D. McQuail, *Media Performance: Mass Communication and the Public Interest*, London: Sage, 1992, p. 76; and J. Lull, *Media, Communication, Culture*, Cambridge: Polity Press, 1995.
3. C. Stevenson, *Ethics and Language*, New Haven, CT: Yale University Press, 1944.
4. S. Fish, *There's No Such Thing as Free Speech*, London: Oxford University Press, 1994.
5. J. Tulloch, *Television Drama: Agency, Audience and Myth*, London: Routledge, 1990; and J. Fiske, *Television Culture*, Routledge: London, 1987.
6. F. Sibley, 'Aesthetic concepts', *Philosophical Review* 67 (1959), pp. 421–50. Philosophic concern with this subject is usually dated to Immanuel Kant's *Critique of Aesthetic Judgement* (1790) in which he argues that the 'pure' aesthetic experience consists of 'disinterested' contemplation of an object that 'pleases for its own sake', without reference to reality or to the 'external' ends of utility or morality.
7. This conceptualization of art is indebted to V. Aldrich, *Philosophy of Art*, Englewood Cliffs, NJ: Prentice-Hall, 1963. It differs from the Aestheticism pioneered in nineteenth-century France (Baudelaire, Flaubert, Gautier) and Britain (Pater, Wilde) with its notion of art as self-

sufficient, '*l'art pour l'art*', having no use or moral aim outside its own being, its values being intrinsic.

8. See the essay 'The voice of poetry in the conversation of mankind' in M. Oakeshott, *Rationalism in Politics*, London: Methuen, 1962, pp. 197–247.

9. J. Fiske and J. Hartley, *Reading Television*, London: Methuen, 1978 on the 'bardic' function, especially in relation to television news.

10. Aldrich, *Philosophy of Art*, ch. 4. See also A. Burgess, *Ninety-Nine Novels: The Best in English Since 1939*, London: Allison & Busby, 1984.

11. J. Corner, *Television Form and Public Address*, London: Edward Arnold, 1995, pp. 169–71.

12. Corner, *Television Form and Public Address*, p. 5.

13. On the distinction between the 'channel' and the 'medium' function of television see S. Hall, 'Television as a medium and its relation to culture', Centre for Contemporary Cultural Studies: University of Birmingham, Working Paper, July 1975.

14. J. Feur, 'The concept of "live television": ontology versus ideology' in E. Kaplan (ed.), *Regarding Television*, Los Angeles, CA: American Film Institute/University Publications of America, 1983.

15. W. Ong, *Orality and Literacy*, London: Methuen, 1982; N. Postman, *Amusing Ourselves to Death*, London: Methuen, 1985. For a sharp criticism of the formulaic nature of an increasingly dominant oral culture in German public service broadcasting see the German television dramatist J. Becker, 'Die Worte verschwinden', *Der Spiegel* 2 (1995), pp. 156–62.

16. J. Blumler (ed.), *Television and the Public Interest*, London: Sage, 1992.

17. P. Barwise and A. Ehrenberg, *Television and its Audience*, London: Sage, 1988.

18. J. Ellis, *Visible Fictions*, London: Routledge, 1981.

19. D. Thorburn, 'Television melodrama' in D. Cater and R. Adler (eds), *Television as a Cultural Force*, New York: Praeger, 1976; L. Schulze, 'The made-for-TV movie: industrial practice, cultural form, popular reception' in T. Balio (ed.), *Hollywood in the Age of Television*, London: Routledge, 1990.

20. Ellis, *Visible Fictions*.

21. Ellis, *Visible Fictions*, pp. 126, 143.

22. Ellis, *Visible Fictions*.

23. T. Gitlin, *Inside Prime Time*, New York: Pantheon, 1983, p. 179; Schulze, 'The made-for-TV movie'.

24. H. Newcomb, 'Towards a television aesthetic' in H. Newcomb (ed.), *Television: The Critical View*, London: Oxford University Press, 1987, pp. 614–20.

25. D. Barker, 'Television production techniques as communication', *Critical Studies in Mass Communication*, September 1985, pp. 234–46.

26. See Ellis, *Visible Fictions* for this contrast between television and cinema.
27. For a useful overview of the characteristics of entertainment progammes see Newcomb (ed.), *Television: The Critical View*.
28. Newcomb, 'Towards a television aesthetic'.
29. R. Dyer, 'Entertainment and utopia' in R. Altman (ed.), *Genre: The Musical: A Reader*, London: Routledge, 1981, p. 177.
30. J. Feur, *MTM: Quality Television*, London: British Film Institute, 1985.
31. For the distinction between 'flat' and 'round' characterization see E. M. Forster, *Aspects of the Novel*, London: Penguin, 1927. On plot and dialogue see S. Chatman, *Story and Discourse: Narrative Structure in Fiction and Film*, Ithaca, NY: Cornell University Press, 1980; also R. Scholes and R. Kellogg, *The Nature of Narrative*, London: Oxford University Press, 1966. See also the critique of television's oral culture in Becker, 'Die Worte verschwinden'.
32. Fiske and Hartley, *Reading Television*.
33. For a rather extreme version of the argument that television advertisements are works of art see M. Nava and O. Nava, 'Discriminating or duped? Young people as consumers of advertising/art', *Magazine of Cultural Studies* 1 (1990), pp. 15–21.
34. J. Corner (ed.), *Documentary and the Mass Media*, London: Edward Arnold, 1986.
35. T. Liebes (ed.), *Narrativization of the News*, Hove: Afterhurst, 1994; J. McManus, *Market-Driven Journalism*, London: Sage, 1994.
36. B. Nichols, *Representing Reality*, Bloomington, IN: Indiana University Press, 1991.
37. Aristotle, *On the Art of Poetry*, London: Oxford University Press, 1920. The notion of the poetic as distinct from the referential was taken up by R. Jacobsen, 'Closing statement: linguistics and poetics' in T. Sebeok (ed.), *Style and Language*, Cambridge, MA: MIT Press, 1960.
38. On television drama as art form see G. Brandt (ed.), *British Television Drama in the 1980s*, London: Cambridge University Press, 1993; and D. Thorburn, 'Television melodrama'.
39. M. Bradbury, 'The celluloid collar 6', *The Listener*, 8 April 1988, p. 23.
40. N. Negroponte, *Being Digital*, London: Hodder & Stoughton, 1995. See also D. Bowen, *Multimedia: Now and Down the Line*, London: Bowerdean, 1994.
41. See the Worldview International Lecture by Barry Diller, chairman of QVC, the television home-shopping channel, to the Edinburgh International Television Festival, June 1994.
42. British Broadcasting Corporation, *Extending Choice: The BBC's Role in the New Broadcasting Age*, London: BBC, 1992.

43. British Broadcasting Corporation, *People and Programmes*, London: BBC, 1995.

44. Peacock Committee, *Report of the Committee on Financing the BBC*, London: HMSO, 1986. For an example of this paradigm see C. Veljanovski and W. Bishop, *Choice by Cable: The Economics of a New Era in Television*, London: Institute of Economic Affairs, Hobart Paper 96, 1983.

45. M. Walzer, *Spheres of Justice: A Defence of Pluralism and Equality*, New York: Basic Books, 1983.

46. The significance of domestic institutional arrangements for deregulation is brought out in K. Dyson (ed.), *The Politics of German Regulation*, Aldershot: Dartmouth, 1992.

47. On US corporate manoeuvring in the embryonic multimedia industry see K. Maney, *Megamedia Shakeout: The Inside Story of the Leaders and Losers in the Exploding Communications Industry*, New York: John Wiley, 1995.

48. For insight into the difficulties at Time-Warner see C. Bruck, *Master of the Game*, New York: Simon & Schuster, 1994.

49. A. Neil, lecture to the Royal Television Society, London, 15 June 1995.

50. On this distinction see Oakeshott, 'The voice of poetry in the conversation of mankind'. Note the influences of Aristotle's poetics and Kant's critique of aesthetic judgement.

51. Taken from T. Zeldin, *The French*, London: Fontana, 1984, pp. 335–6.

52. On regulation as 'statecraft' see K. Dyson and P. Humphreys, *Broadcasting and New Media Policies in Western Europe*, London: Routledge, 1988, especially ch. 8.

53. J. Blumler, M. Brynin and T. Nossiter, 'Broadcasting finance and programme quality', *European Journal of Communication* 1(3) (1986), pp. 343–64.

54. B. Williams, '"North to the future": *Northern Exposure* and quality television', *The Spectator*, USC School of Film and Television, 1993.

Index